MEMORY, 2008, 16 (1), 1–2

Psychology Press
Taylor & Francis Group

Editorial

New insights in trauma and memory: A special issue of *Memory*

Elke Geraerts
Maastricht University, the Netherlands, and Harvard University, Cambridge, MA, USA

Marko Jelicic
Maastricht University, the Netherlands

How people remember—and forget—traumatic experiences is a highly controversial issue in psychiatry and psychology. At the moment, the field of trauma and memory is dominated by several controversies (for reviews, see Brewin, 2007; McNally, 2003; Zoellner & Bittenger, 2004). One prominent controversy pertains to the authenticity of reports of "recovered memories" of childhood sexual abuse (CSA). Some scholars and clinicians maintain that the mind can protect itself by repressing traumatic events from awareness. Others hold that abuse, combat, and other horrifying events are seemingly imprinted in memory and are seldom, if ever, truly forgotten. Thus some authors claim that it is possible to recover memories that have been inaccessible for many years, whereas others remain sceptical about the veracity of such recovered memories. There is also debate about the nature of memory for traumatic experiences (see, e.g., Geraerts et al., 2007). A number of authors argue that there are qualitative differences between traumatic and non-traumatic memories. They contend that traumatic memory can only be explained by postulating special memory mechanisms. Others disagree and state that no special memory system is needed to explain this type of memory. In their eyes, remembering traumatic experiences is governed by basic laws of memory. A related controversy has to do with the malleability of traumatic memory. Several authors opine that because traumatic experiences are burned into memory, recollections of trauma would be largely resistant to distortions. Again, others disagree and stress that traumatic memory is just as malleable as non-traumatic memory.

The purpose of this special issue of *Memory* is to highlight studies examining remembering and forgetting in people who report having experienced traumatic events. Moreover, this issue will also focus on research manipulating memory functioning, thereby providing us with important information regarding the status of traumatic memories. The special issue opens with three papers reporting research in people who have experienced traumatic events like combat or sexual abuse. Iris Engelhard and colleagues report a prospective study examining the consistency of retrospective accounts of traumatic events reported by Dutch soldiers deployed to Iraq. This theme is continued by Kristine Peace and co-workers, who compare characteristics of traumatic memories for sexual violence with other types of emotional experiences. Finally, Elke Geraerts and colleagues examine memory functioning in people who report that they have

Address correspondence to: Elke Geraerts, Department of Psychology, Harvard University, 1232 William James Hall, 33 Kirkland Street, Cambridge, MA 02138, USA. E-mail: E.Geraerts@Psychology.Unimaas.NL

http://www.psypress.com/memory DOI:10.1080/09658210701722895

forgotten being sexually abused as a child, only to recover it later in life. In this study, they examine links between attempted suppression of autobiographical memories and recovered CSA memories.

Next, Kamala London and colleagues critically review literature on retrospective accounts from adults reporting CSA experiences from their childhood, as well as studies of children undergoing forensic evaluation for CSA.

The second theme in this special issue relates to manipulation of memory functioning to address questions in the field of trauma and memory. Nicoline Hall and Dorthe Berntsen examine the effect of emotional stress on voluntary and involuntary (intrusive) memories. Next, two other papers study the effects of manipulation on memory accuracy and the creation of false memories. Pedro Paz-Alonso and Gail Goodman examine adults' memory for a distressing film. They explore the effects of providing misinformation, changing the order of retrieval and the retention interval. Relatedly, James Ost and coworkers examine whether media exposure (and hence familiarity) could lead to an increase in memory distortions regarding the terrorist attacks in London (7 July 2005).

Given the current debate on trauma and memory, findings and principles emerging from studies with survivors of traumatic events, but also from laboratory studies concerning memory functioning, are essential for evaluating claims about the special status of traumatic memory. In our view, research on trauma and memory may provide important clues to the architecture and characteristics of both abnormal *and* normal memory functioning. We hope that the articles in this special issue of *Memory* will be helpful in resolving some of the controversies in the field of trauma and memory.

REFERENCES

Brewin, C. R. (2007). Autobiographical memory for trauma: Update on four controversies. *Memory, 15*, 227–248.

Geraerts, E., Kozaric-Kovacic, D., Merckelbach, H., Peraica, T., Jelicic, M., & Candel, I. (2007). Traumatic memories in war veterans: Not so special after all. *Consciousness and Cognition, 16*, 170–177.

McNally, R. J. (2003). *Remembering trauma*. Cambridge, MA: Belknap Press/Harvard University Press.

Zoellner, L. A., & Bittenger, J. N. (2004). On the uniqueness of trauma memories in PTSD. In G. M. Rosen (Ed.), *Posttraumatic stress disorder: Issues and controversies* (pp. 147–162). New York: John Wiley Press.

Psychology Press
Taylor & Francis Group

Memory consistency for traumatic events in Dutch soldiers deployed to Iraq

Iris M. Engelhard and Marcel A. van den Hout
Utrecht University, Utrecht, The Netherlands

Richard J. McNally
Harvard University, Cambridge, MA, USA

Retrospective accounts of traumatic events are consistently associated with symptoms of post-traumatic stress disorder (PTSD). This has often been interpreted as *causal* impact of such events on psychological functioning, but recent studies suggest that the causal direction is (partly) reversed: high levels of PTSD symptoms may be associated with amplified recollections of precipitating traumatic events. The aim of this prospective study was to index the consistency with which Dutch Army soldiers reported traumatic stressors and nontraumatic stressors on their deployment to Iraq, and to examine to what extent PTSD symptoms and pre-existing reporting biases, such as that arising from neuroticism, affect memory inconsistency. Retrospective accounts of stressors were highly variable over time. Individuals with higher levels of PTSD symptoms and neuroticism, lower levels of extraversion, and fewer prior missions, were more prone to increased reporting over time.

The frequency and severity of post-traumatic stress disorder (PTSD) symptoms usually vary as a function of stressor severity (e.g., Dohrenwend et al., 2006; Hoge et al., 2004; Hotopf et al., 2006). Despite exceptions to this dose–response rule (McNally, 2003, pp. 79–100), in general, the more severe the trauma, the more severe the post-traumatic morbidity. Although this association is often interpreted as confirming the casual impact of stressor severity on functioning, one cannot infer causation from correlation. In fact, most studies documenting the dose–response effect are based on retrospective recollection of trauma severity among individuals with PTSD. This is problematic because clinical status can affect how one remembers one's traumatic experiences (e.g., King et al., 2000; Roemer, Litz, Orsillo, Ehlich, & Friedman, 1998; Schwarz, Kowalski, & McNally, 1993; Southwick, Morgan, Nicolaou, & Charney, 1997; Wessely et al., 2003).

The worse the current symptoms, the more severe individuals remember their trauma to have been. For example, school workers were asked to complete a questionnaire about their memory for a fatal shooting at an elementary school 6 months earlier (Schwarz et al., 1993). The questionnaire was re-administered 18 months after the shooting. Severity of PTSD symptoms at 18 months predicted participants' remembering the event as worse than they did at 6 months. Those doing better at follow-up tended to remember the event

Address correspondence to: Iris M. Engelhard PhD, Clinical and Health Psychology, Utrecht University, PO Box 80140, 3508 TC Utrecht, The Netherlands. E-mail: i.m.engelhard@uu.nl

This study was supported by a grant from the Veterans Institute (Doorn, The Netherlands) and an Innovational Research Incentive VENI Scheme (016.045.106) of the Netherlands Organisation for Scientific Research awarded to Iris M. Engelhard. We thank representatives of the Netherlands Ministry of Defence for their cooperation, and the commanders and soldiers who participated in this study for their service. We also thank Ron M. Rapee for helpful comments about a presentation of an earlier draft of this paper.

http://www.psypress.com/memory DOI:10.1080/09658210701334022

as less disturbing than they had earlier. Likewise, Gulf War veterans were asked to complete questionnaires concerning their exposure to war-related stressors 1 month and 2 years after their deployment (Southwick et al., 1997). Severity of PTSD symptoms at 2 years predicted the number of traumatic events reported at 2 years that were not reported at 1 month.

These studies have methodological limitations. First, participants had already been traumatised when they enrolled in the study. The most serious problem with this is that it is possible that those who most strongly attribute symptoms to traumatic events will be most likely to participate in a study that asks about both (Hotopf & Wessely, 2005). The result could be an overestimation of the extent of retrospective recall bias. To avoid selective sampling, researchers should recruit individuals at risk for exposure to trauma (such as soldiers) and then follow them over time. But such prospective studies are rarely feasible. Second, earlier studies focused on the frequency of traumatic events, but few studies tested to what extent PTSD symptoms are related to inconsistent recall of the emotional *impact* of the event at the time. This is an important issue because subjective appraisal of stressor severity is often more predictive of PTSD than are objective measures of stressor severity (Bowman, 1999). It is also unclear whether memory for nontraumatic stressors, such as daily difficulties (e.g., for soldiers on deployment this could be irritations and pressures within a malevolent or harsh war zone, such as lack of privacy, having to endure the climate, etc.), is also vulnerable to distortion as a function of current clinical state. Finally, due to the retrospective nature of prior studies, little is known about pre-trauma predictors for memory distortions. Some of these variables may be assessed post-trauma, such as the number of earlier missions that either may act as a vulnerability factor or may make soldiers resilient. Other pre-trauma variables, such as prior life events, neuroticism, and extraversion, would have to be assessed before trauma, as post-trauma assessments may affect scores. For example, the presence of PTSD symptoms may inflate neuroticism scores due to item overlap (Engelhard, van den Hout, & Kindt, 2003)

In this study, we administered self-report measures of traumatic stressors and nontraumatic stressors to Dutch soldiers who were deployed to Iraq. They completed these measures 5 months and 15 months after their deployment. The participants were recruited prior to deployment. The aims of this study were to investigate: (1) the stability of memories for stressors and their emotional impact over time, (2) the association between variability in these reports and symptoms of PTSD, and (3) pre-trauma predictors of variability. This report is part of a larger project on experimental approaches to PTSD (e.g., Engelhard, Huijding, van den Hout, & de Jong, 2007; Engelhard & van den Hout, 2007).

METHOD

Participants

A total of 216 infantry troops of the Royal Netherlands Army were asked to participate in this study prior to their 4-month tour in the peacekeeping mission in Iraq in 2004. They were recruited on the basis of availability during preparations for Iraq, from one rotation and several units. Participation was voluntary. After the research team had given the participants a complete oral and written description of the study, written informed consent was obtained. This was done both before and after deployment. Just 2 soldiers refused, and 214 (5% female) agreed to participate, and completed questionnaires assessing prior missions, prior life events, neuroticism, and extraversion, about 6 weeks before their deployment. Their mean age was 23.1 ($SD = 4.5$). Most were single, and 22% were married or cohabiting. The majority had finished high school, 7% only finished elementary school, and 2% were college educated. For nearly two-thirds this was their first peacekeeping mission, 24% had completed 1 prior mission, and 15% had completed 2 or 3 prior missions. About 5 months after their deployment, 171 (80%) of the participants completed questionnaires about traumatic stressors and nontraumatic stressors in Iraq and PTSD symptoms. At about 15 months, 152 soldiers (response rate: 152/217 = 71%) completed these same questionnaires; 133 of them completed all questionnaires at 5 months and at 15 months. Most of the assessments took place at the base, but at 15 months about a third of the participants were tested via mail. The university Institutional Review Board approved this study.

Measures

Prior life events were measured with a 17-item checklist that included road accidents, sudden death of a loved one, fire, being robbed, or being threatened with a weapon. A count of all endorsed items was used. Neuroticism and extraversion were assessed with the Eysenck Personality Questionnaire (EPQ; Eysenck & Eysenck, 1975). The Potentially Traumatising Events Scale (PTES; Maguen, Litz, Wang, & Cook, 2004) includes 21 potentially traumatic war-zone stressors (e.g., going on patrols, disarming civilians, being shot at), and the General Overseas Mission Stressors and Negative Peacekeeping Experiences Scale (Maguen et al., 2004) includes 30 nontraumatic stressors (e.g., feeling bored, being unable to identify a clear enemy, feeling unclear about what to do in threatening situations, difficulties getting mail, bad weather conditions). We omitted one item from the PTES because it was already included in the nontraumatic stressors scale (i.e., patrolling areas where there were land mines, added two items) for the Iraq mission (item 1 and 21, Table 1), and rewrote two nontraumatic stressors in general terms (in the original scale, these referred to civilians in Kosovo, which we rephrased as "civilians"). For each item, participants indicated whether they had experienced it, and if so how much of a negative impact it had on them at the time of the event (1 = no impact, 2 = little negative, 3 = moderately negative, 4 = extremely negative). For both types of stressors, we calculated the number of endorsed items and the number of items rated as "moderately" or "extremely" negative. PTSD symptoms were measured with the PTSD Symptom Scale (PSS-SR; Foa, Riggs, Dancu, & Rothbaum, 1993), which includes the 17 PTSD symptoms that are rated on a 4-point severity scale (0 = not at all, 3 = almost always). Ratings were summed to yield a PTSD symptom severity score.

RESULTS

Stability

The correlation between the number of potentially traumatic stressors recalled at 5 and 15

TABLE 1
Potentially traumatic stressors in Iraq organised by the highest change in responses

	Participants' responses					
					Change	
	YY	*YN*	*NY*	*NN*	*n*	%
1. Having injured civilians due to own action	16	29	20	68	49	37
2. Seeing dead or injured NATO (non-Dutch) soldiers	16	22	16	79	38	29
3. Fear that you might be taken hostage	81	18	18	16	36	27
4. Seeing human remains	21	16	18	78	34	26
5. Seeing dead or injured civilians	48	7	25	53	32	24
6. Having to aid in the removal of unexploded ordnance	10	16	16	91	32	24
7. Needing to manage civilians in chaotic conditions	74	13	16	30	29	22
8. Patrolling through the zone of separation	56	17	10	50	27	20
9. Seeing dead or injured Dutch soldiers	52	13	13	55	26	20
10. Having to aid in the removal of human remains	3	15	11	104	26	20
11. Being shot at	75	6	19	33	25	19
12. Locating unexploded land mines	12	9	15	97	24	18
13. Witnessing an explosion	90	14	9	20	23	17
14. Being injured because of an assault/attack	5	14	5	109	19	14
15. Witnessing violence	100	13	5	15	18	14
16. Experienced sexual harassment during deployment	3	11	3	116	14	11
17. Being injured because of an accident	9	8	6	110	14	11
18. Disarming civilians	86	4	8	36	12	9
19. Fear of having your unit fired on	120	7	4	2	11	8
20. Fear of being ambushed or attacked	127	3	4	0	7	5
21. Being informed of a Dutch soldier who got killed	126	0	6	1	6	5
22. Going on patrols or performing other dangerous duties	116	4	2	12	6	5

YY = endorsed at both time points, YN = no longer endorsed, NY = newly endorsed, NN = not endorsed at either time point.

months was $r(133) = 0.64$, $p < .001$. The mean number of events did not change significantly over time, $t(132) = 0.26$, *NS*. Following Southwick et al. (1997), we created variables indicating whether the event was either endorsed at both times (YY); at 5 months, but not at 15 months (YN); not endorsed at 5 months, but endorsed at 15 months (NY); or never endorsed (NN; see Table 1). A total of 80% reported at least one YN change, and 47% reported two or more changes. Similarly, 70% reported at least one NY change, and 45% reported two or more. Interestingly, the NY category contained not only new recollections of subjective experiences, such as "fear that you might be taken hostage" (see Table 1, item 3), but also relatively objective events like "seeing dead or injured civilians" (item 5) or "being shot at" (item 11).

The correlation between the number of events recalled as negative at 5 and 15 months was $r(133) = 0.55$, $p < .001$. The mean number of negative events did not change over time either, $t(132) = 0.55$, *NS*. About 52% reported at least one change from "not negative" to "negative", and 47% reported at least one change in the opposite direction. Items that changed most often from "not negative" to "negative" were: being told about a colleague who got killed (22%), fear of being ambushed (15%), witnessing an explosion (11%), and being shot at (11%). The former three items also changed most often the other way around (8–16%).

The correlation between the number of non-traumatic stressors recalled at 5 and 15 months was $r(135) = 0.65$, $p < .001$, and the mean scores decreased over time, $t(134) = 3.59$, $p < .001$. A total of 79% reported at least one YN change, and 67% reported at least one NY change. The most common YN items were: seeing kids who had been victims of violence (25%), not understanding the unit's mission (21%), and having to remain neutral in the face of conflicts between civilians (20%). The most common NY items were: frustration about not knowing what to do with captured insurgents (15%), patrolling areas where there were land mines (13%), and lack of clarity about what to do in threatening situations (13%).

The correlation between the number of non-traumatic events recalled as moderately or extremely negative at 5 and 15 months was $r(135) = 0.67$, $p < .001$. Again, the mean scores dropped over time, $t(134) = 2.34$, $p = .02$. The items most often changed from "negative" to "not negative" included frustration with terrorist activity (16%), civilians having hostile reactions while you were trying to help (16%), being unable to identify a clear enemy (15%), and knowing that many war criminals were not arrested (14%). These were equally changed the other way around (14–16%).

Associations with PTSD symptoms and pre-trauma variables

The PSS and change scores were non-normally distributed and were transformed with square root to increase normality. Change in PTSD symptoms (15 months minus 5 months) was used to test for associations with variations in self-reported experiences. To obtain a graphical representation of the data, we divided participants into a PTSD-positive group ($n = 21$) and a PTSD-negative group ($n = 112$), defined by PSS criteria for PTSD at 15 months[1] (see Figures 1 and 2). Figure 1 suggests that the PTSD group show increases in their reporting of traumatic stressors, whereas the other group did not. In fact, worsening of PTSD symptoms at 15 months was significantly related to more NY changes in traumatic events, $r(133) = 0.18$, $p = .04$, but it was unrelated to YN changes, $r(133) = -0.07$. It was also related to more NY changes in events with a negative impact at the time, $r(133) = 0.23$, $p = .01$, and to fewer YN changes in such events, $r(133) = -0.24$, $p = .01$ (Figure 2). Worsening of PTSD symptoms was related to more NY changes in *non-traumatic* events with a negative impact, $r(133) = 0.24$, $p = .01$, but it was not significantly related to any other change in recall of non-traumatic events (largest $r = -0.13$ for forgetting of difficulties), although the correlations were in the same direction (i.e., positive for NY changes and negative for YN changes).

Prior missions, prior life events, neuroticism, and extraversion were correlated with the inconsistency variables that were significantly linked to PTSD symptoms. The only significant correlation for traumatic events was between NY changes in events recalled as negative and neuroticism, $r(132) = 0.19$, $p = .03$. A regression analysis

[1] This is a symptom-based PTSD definition that follows DSM-IV criteria but does not include impairment (i.e., at least one re-experiencing symptom, three avoidance symptoms, and two hyperarousal symptoms had to be rated at least "some of the time"; Foa et al., 1993).

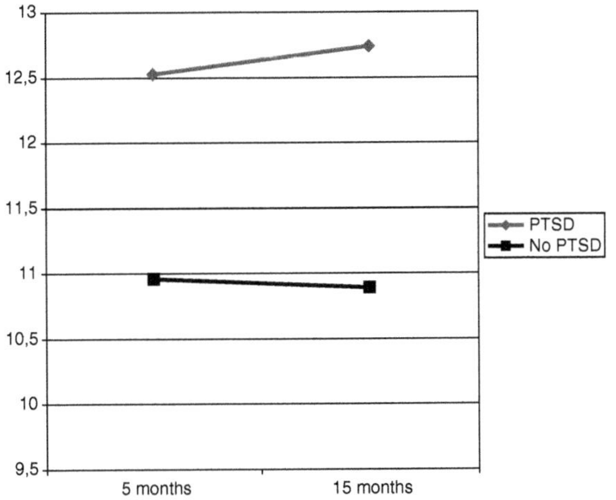

Figure 1. The number of potentially traumatic stressors recalled at 5 and 15 months.

showed that worsening of PTSD symptoms, $\beta = 0.22$, $t = 2.64$, $p < .01$, and higher neuroticism $\beta = 0.16$, $t = 1.90$, $p = .06$, predicted the number of NY changes, $F(2, 129) = 6.11$, $p < .01$, $R^2 = .09$. NY changes in non-traumatic events recalled as negative were related to neuroticism, $r(134) = 0.25$, $p < .01$, extraversion, $r(134) = -0.22$, $p = .01$, and prior missions, $r(135) = -0.19$, $p = .03$. A regression analysis showed that worsening of PTSD symptoms, $\beta = 0.21$, $t = 2.54$, $p = .01$, lower extraversion, $\beta = -0.25$, $t = 3.01$, $p < .01$, and fewer prior missions, $\beta = -0.18$, $t = 2.19$, $p = .03$, predicted more NY changes in non-traumatic events recalled as negative, $F(3, 128) = 7.13$, $p < .001$, $R^2 = 0.14$, but neuroticism was no longer significant, $\beta = 0.14$, $t = 1.54$, $p = .13$.

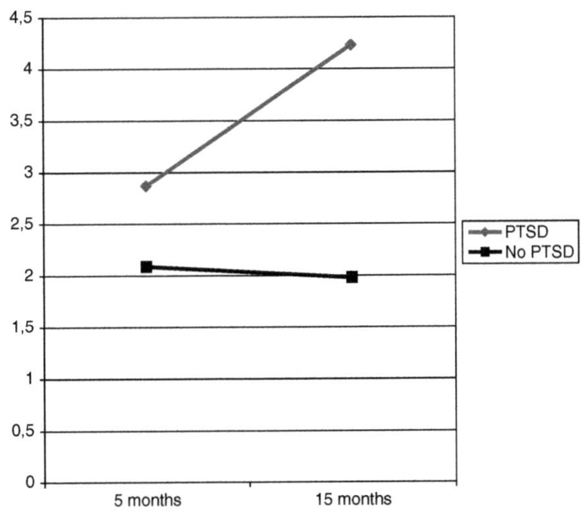

Figure 2. The number of potentially traumatic stressors recalled as negative.

DISCUSSION

In line with other studies, retrospective accounts of trauma exposure were variable over time. This inconsistency occurred for a wide variety of events, but most referred to specific, nontrivial events, such as seeing human remains, being injured because of an attack, and being shot at. Similar inconsistencies occurred for lower-magnitude stressors (e.g., having difficulty getting mail, lack of clarity about what to do in threatening situations). In addition, the more a participant reported PTSD symptoms, the more he or she retrospectively increased reporting of both traumatic stressors and nontraumatic stressors occurring during their deployment in Iraq. If psychiatrically ill, traumatised individuals remember traumatic events as worse than they originally did, this will inflate post-trauma estimates of the dose–response relationship between trauma and symptoms. We also found that those who are well were more inclined to forget the negative *impact* of such events. We did not verify the actual occurrences of traumatic events and therefore do not know which of the two time points depicts a more accurate representation of the truth. However, the focus of this study was on changes in reporting of memories.

Inconsistencies in reporting autobiographical memory are not uncommon. The question is why a specific memory change (NY changes) is associated with particular psychological problems (PTSD symptoms). The most likely explanation is that increased reports may result from a reappraisal process: those who suffer from more problems may try most strongly to make sense of their problems and attribute them to deployment-related stressors. Events previously seen as irrelevant and not endorsed may have increased in importance over time, and may be labelled differently (e.g., a person calling the sight of blood "seeing human remains"). It is also possible that individuals with more symptoms are more unwilling or unable to make efforts that are necessary to figure out exactly whether experiences occurred to them. They may retrieve less-specific representations of what occurred during their deployment, and may rely more on gist. Vague impressions of similarity between an item and a past event may result in false recognition. At least among war veterans, PTSD is related to deficits in retrieving specific memories (McNally, Litz, Prassas, Shin, & Weathers, 1994). Finally, increases in item endorsement may be explained by new information and source memory errors. New knowledge about deployment to Iraq from whatever source (e.g., unit meetings, media) may get inadvertently incorporated into one's autobiographical memories of deployment. Possibly, post-mission information is more salient for PTSD sufferers, making it likely that the new information gets integrated in autobiographical memory. If memory about new information contains perceptual details about the context or setting, individuals are inclined to believe it is a real memory for an actual event (Johnson, Hashtroudi, & Lindsay, 1993).

The findings are consistent with other studies (e.g., Southwick et al., 1997) showing that retrospective accounts of traumatic events are not necessarily veridical. The magnitude of the link between PTSD symptoms and changes in reports of stressors is small, but noteworthy: individuals with more symptoms tend to amplify their memories of major and more minor stressors over time. With regard to clinical care, clinicians often conclude that the trauma reported to them by the patient is accurate and genuine. It is important for clinicians to understand that memory for a potentially traumatic event is not immutable. The very notion that PTSD is strongly related to stressor exposure is mainly based on correlations between self-reports about current symptoms and earlier events. The fact that self-reports about earlier events are influenced by symptoms seems relevant to the validity of the PTSD concept: when retrospective self-reports are used, the phenomenon of state-dependent memory retrieval will serve to overestimate the relationship between aversive events and PTSD symptoms. As Young (2004) has emphasised, the concept of PTSD has an "inner logic" (p. 128) whereby the memory of an event is the source of subsequent symptoms. According to this received view of PTSD, the symptoms themselves should not work backward, so to speak, and alter the memory. Yet this clearly does happen, underscoring the dynamic and malleable character of traumatic memory.

Manuscript received 15 December 2006
Manuscript accepted 13 March 2007
First published online 14 May 2007

REFERENCES

Bowman, M. L. (1999). Individual differences in post-traumatic distress: Problems with the DSM-IV model. *Canadian Journal of Psychiatry, 44*, 21–33.

Dohrenwend, B. P., Turner, J. B., Turse, N. A., Adams, B. G., Koenen, K. C., & Marshall, R. (2006). The psychological risks of Vietnam for U.S. Veterans: A revisit with new data and methods. *Science, 313*, 979–982.

Engelhard, I. M., Huijding, J., van den Hout, M. A., & de Jong, P. J. (2007). Vulnerability associations and symptoms of post-traumatic stress disorder after deployment to Iraq. *Behavior Research and Therapy, 45*, 2317–2325.

Engelhard, I. M., & van den Hout, M. A. (2007). Pre-existing neuroticism, stressor severity, and post traumatic stress in soldiers deployed to Iraq. *Canadian Journal of Psychiatry, 52*, 505–509.

Engelhard, I. M., van den Hout, M. A., & Kindt, M. (2003). The relationship between neuroticism, pre-traumatic stress, and post-traumatic stress: A prospective study. *Personality and Individual Differences, 35*, 381–388.

Eysenck, H. J., & Eysenck, S. B. G. (1975). *Manual of the Eysenck Personality Questionnaire.* San Diego, CA: Educational and Industrial Testing Service.

Foa, E. B., Riggs, D. S., Dancu, C. V., & Rothbaum, B. O. (1993). Reliability and validity of a brief instrument for assessing post-traumatic stress disorder. *Journal of Traumatic Stress, 6*, 459–473.

Hoge, C. W., Castro, C. A., & Messer, S. C., McGurk, D., Cotting, D. I., & Koffman, R. L. (2004). Combat duty in Iraq and Afghanistan, mental health problems, and barriers to care. *New England Journal of Medicine, 351*, 13–22.

Hotopf, M., Hull, L., Fear, N. T., Browne, T., Horn, O., Iversen, A., et al. (2006). The health of UK military personnel who deployed to the 2003 Iraq war: A cohort study. *The Lancet, 367*, 1731–1741.

Hotopf, M., & Wessely, S. (2005). Can epidemiology clear the fog of war? Lessons from the 1990–91 Gulf War. *International Journal of Epidemiology, 34*, 791–800.

Johnson, M. K., Hashtroudi, S., & Lindsay, D. S. (1993). Source monitoring. *Psychological Bulletin, 114*, 3–28.

King, D. W., King, L. A., Erickson, D. J., Huang, M. T., Sharkansky, E. J., & Wolfe, J. (2000). Post-traumatic stress disorder and retrospectively reported stressor exposure: A longitudinal prediction model. *Journal of Abnormal Psychology, 109*, 624–633.

Maguen, S., Litz, B. T., Wang, J. L., & Cook, M. (2004). The stressors and demands of peacekeeping in Kosovo: Predictors of mental health response. *Military Medicine, 169*, 198–206.

McNally, R. J. (2003). *Remembering trauma.* Cambridge, MA: Harvard University Press.

McNally, R. J., Litz, B. T., Prassas, A., Shin, L. M., & Weathers, F. W. (1994). Emotional priming of autobiographical memory in post-traumatic stress disorder. *Cognition and Emotion, 8*, 351–367.

Roemer, L., Litz, B. T., Orsillo, S. M., Ehlich, P. J., & Friedman, M. J. (1998). Increases in retrospective accounts of war-zone exposure over time: The role of PTSD symptom severity. *Journal of Traumatic Stress, 11*, 597–605.

Schwarz, E. D., Kowalski, J. M., & McNally, R. J. (1993). Malignant memories: Post-traumatic changes in memory in adults after a school shooting. *Journal of Traumatic Stress, 6*, 545–553.

Southwick, S. M., Morgan, C. A. III, Nicolaou, A. L., & Charney, D. S. (1997). Consistency of memory for combat-related traumatic events in veterans of Operation Desert Storm. *American Journal of Psychiatry, 154*, 173–177.

Wessely, S., Unwin, C., Hotopf, M., Hull, L., Ismail, K., Nicolaou, V., et al. (2003). Stability of recall of military hazards over time. *British Journal of Psychiatry, 183*, 314–322.

Young, A. (2004). When traumatic memory was a problem: On the historical antecedents of PTSD. In G. M. Rosen (Ed.), *Post-traumatic stress disorder: Issues and controversies* (pp. 127–146). Chichester, UK: Wiley.

MEMORY, 2008, 16 (1), 10–21

Psychology Press
Taylor & Francis Group

Are memories for sexually traumatic events "special"? A within-subjects investigation of trauma and memory in a clinical sample

Kristine A. Peace
Grant MacEwan College, Edmonton, AB, Canada

Stephen Porter and Leanne ten Brinke
Dalhousie University, Halifax, NS, Canada

According to a long-standing clinical tradition, sexually traumatic experiences are processed and recalled differently from other experiences, often leading to memory impairment. In this study, we compared the characteristics of traumatic memories for sexual violence and two other types of emotional experiences. $N = 44$ women recruited from a local sexual trauma agency were asked to recall and describe three autobiographical events: sexual abuse/assault, a non-sexual trauma, and a positive emotional event. The characteristics of the three memory types were compared on both subjective and objective measures. Further, the potential influences of level of traumatic impact and dissociation were assessed. Results indicated that memories for sexual trauma were not impaired or fragmented relative to other memories. Instead, memories for sexual trauma were associated with a remarkably high level of vividness, detail, and sensory components. Further, high levels of traumatic impact were not associated with memory impairment. Implications for the ongoing traumatic memory debate are discussed.

Although the relation between trauma and memory has been the focus of psychological research for many years, there still is little consensus concerning how traumatic events are processed and recalled (e.g., McNally, 2003). A range of perspectives have been applied to understanding the impact of trauma on memory, from the traditional clinical argument that trauma impairs memory for the event (e.g., Brewin, 2001; Hyman & Byrne, 1999; Nadel & Jacobs, 1998; van der Kolk & Fisler, 1995) to the increasingly supported scientific view that memory is facilitated by trauma (e.g., Berntsen, 2001; Porter & Peace, in press). For example, Porter and Peace (in press) asked participants to recall a recent traumatic experience and a positive emotional experience in interviews separated by 3 months (see Peace & Porter, 2004) and again after 3.45 to 5 years. Traumatic experiences were more enduring over time than positive experiences, both in terms of vividness and factual consistency.

Studies of extreme trauma, such as the experience of a concentration camp in World War II, also suggest that traumatic memories can be

Address correspondence to: Kristine A. Peace PhD, Department of Psychology, Grant MacEwan College, City Centre Campus, Rm 6–329, 10700–104 Avenue, Edmonton, AB, Canada, T5J 4S2. E-mail: PeaceK@macewan.ca

The authors would like to thank the Social Sciences and Humanities Research Council of Canada (SSHRC) (operating grant to the second author) and the American Psychology-Law Society (APLS) (doctoral grant to the first author) for providing funding assistance with this project. We would also like to thank the Avalon Sexual Assault Centre (specifically Myrna Carlson) and the individual psychologists in the local community who assisted in recruiting participants from their clientele. In addition, the research assistance of Naomi Doucette and Allison Eisner was greatly appreciated. Finally, we would like to thank the sexual assault victims who shared the depths of their experiences for this research.

http://www.psypress.com/memory DOI:10.1080/09658210701363583

remarkably enduring (e.g., Merckelbach, Dekkers, Wessel, & Roefs, 2003; Schelach & Nachson, 2001; Wagenaar & Groeneweg, 1990). Recent research examining traumatic experiences in Croatian war veterans suffering from PTSD demonstrated that memory for trauma remained stable over time and was recalled similarly to neutral events (Geraerts et al., 2007). Collectively, these studies indicate that recollections of trauma typically are not impaired relative to other emotional and non-emotional events. Perhaps a more contentious remaining issue is whether specific types of traumas may lead to impairment. In particular, sexual trauma often is viewed as having a unique impact on memory, generally such that it is recalled more poorly than other traumatic experiences (e.g., Koss, Figueredo, Bell, Tharan, & Tromp, 1996) due to dissociation or repression. The goals of the present study were to examine: (1) the characteristics of memories of sexual victimisation relative to other traumatic and non-traumatic events; (2) the impact of level of trauma on memory quality; and (3) the possible association of alexithymia and dissociation with memory impairment.

IS SEXUAL TRAUMA UNIQUE?

Relative to other traumatic experiences, sexual assault in adulthood is associated with one of the highest rates of post-traumatic stress disorder (PTSD), while child sexual abuse (CSA) is associated with more varied reactions (e.g., Foa & Rothbaum, 1998; Hanson et al., 2001, Rind, Tromovitch, & Bauserman, 1998; Schiraldi, 2000). On the surface, some studies are consistent with the notion that sexual trauma is associated with incomplete memories. For example, Williams (1994) reported that approximately 38% of women with documented cases of CSA failed to recall these specific incidents in adulthood. Interpretations of this finding are varied, including that the women simply chose not to acknowledge and discuss the events with the researcher (see Ofshe & Watters, 1994).

Koss and colleagues found that rape memories (and traumatic memories in general) subjectively were less vivid, less coherent, less detailed, more poorly remembered, and generally avoided in thought and discussion (e.g., Koss et al., 1996; Koss, Figueredo, Bell, Tharan, & Tromp, 1999; Tromp, Koss, Figueredo, & Tharan, 1995) relative to memories for other types of emotional events. However, this research involved a mail-out survey and respondents were simply asked to respond to questions about qualities of their memories for a rape, an "unpleasant", or a "pleasant" experience, but were not asked to provide a narrative description of the events. Griesel, Cooper, Hernandez, and Yuille (2005) examined memories of sexual trauma and positive experiences in sex-trade workers. Their findings revealed that sexual assaults and positive events showed similar patterns of memory characteristics in both the quantity and quality of details. Thus, memory for sexual trauma did not appear to be impaired, but neither did it appear to be dissimilar from other types of emotional events. Porter and Birt (2001) reported that in comparison to memories for non-sexual traumatic experiences, memories for sexual trauma were associated with higher levels of vividness and clarity, had more sensory components, and were rated as having a higher overall quality. On the other hand, Berliner, Hyman, Thomas, and Fitzgerald (2003) found that memories for sexual (relative to non-sexual) traumas among children were less vivid, less coherent, and contained less sensory detail. The researchers suggested that the repeated nature of sexually abusive experiences might have affected recall for particular episodes. Nonetheless, based on their overall findings, the authors observed that "trauma memories (both sexual and non-sexual) and memories for positive events are more similar than not" (p. 235). Other work suggests that CSA memories can remain detailed and reliable over long periods. For example, Alexander et al. (2005) found that memories for documented CSA were generally highly detailed and enduring, even over extended intervals (e.g., 12 to 21 years). Thus, while some research supports that sexual trauma may lead to impaired memory functioning, other studies find no evidence for memory impairment relative to other experiences.

THE INFLUENCE OF LEVEL OF TRAUMATIC IMPACT

Another controversy in the area of trauma and memory concerns whether the degree of trauma influences memory quality. For example, clinical levels of PTSD have been linked to autobiographical memory impairments (Brewin, 2001; Halligan, Michael, Clark, & Ehlers, 2003). The extent to which the event is re-experienced in memory through vivid flashbacks and intrusions of the event, as well as subsequent attempts to avoid recall, may lead to difficulties in intentional recall about the traumatic episodes (e.g., Byrne, Hyman, & Scott, 2001; Tromp et al., 1995). As such, some have argued that extreme traumatic memories lack integration in consciousness and do not contain a coherent narrative, instead being experienced mainly as sensory and emotional fragments (Brewin, Dalgleish, & Joseph, 1996). However, these effects may not be maintained over time, as traumatic impact tends to subside independently over time and/or with treatment for PSTD. Accordingly, a reduction in trauma symptomatology has been associated with improved memory for the event.

Foa, Molnar, and Cashman (1995) studied memories for rape experiences both before and after exposure therapy. They found that memories were more coherent and less fragmented after therapy, suggesting that higher levels of traumatic stress impaired recall but that these deficits are not permanent. While some studies have linked traumatic stress to memory dysfunction (e.g., Tromp et al., 1995), other empirical evidence suggests that clinical levels of stress are associated with a different (but not impaired) pattern of recollection (e.g., Geraerts et al., 2007; Roemer, Litz, Orsillo, Ehlich, & Friedman, 1998; Rubin, Feldman, & Beckham, 2004; see also McNally, 2003). For example, Berntsen, Willert, and Rubin (2003) evaluated traumatic memories associated with PTSD versus those that were not linked to PTSD. Overall, memories recalled by the PTSD group were no more fragmented than the non-PSTD group. Higher levels of traumatic impact were associated with a higher degree of vividness, detail, emotion, and sensory information (Berntsen et al., 2003). In their sample, Porter and Birt (2001) evaluated memory characteristics as a function of trauma severity and found that severe traumatic events were associated with greater vividness and clarity in memory as compared to traumatic events with lower stress levels (also see Alexander et al., 2005).

THE ROLE OF ALEXITHYMIA AND DISSOCIATION IN TRAUMATIC REMEMBERING

It is possible that individual pathological responses to sexual trauma may be associated with emotional processing deficits that impair subsequent recollections. Alexithymia refers to a condition in which an individual continually has difficulty in recognising and describing their emotional experiences (Kenny, 1998; Lumley, Gustavson, Partridge, & Labouvie-Vief, 2005), and difficulty discriminating between emotional states and bodily sensations (Taylor, 1984). Taylor, Bagby, and Parker (1997) reported that alexithymic individuals may have difficulty in associating feelings with memories, which could lead to impaired recollections. Several studies have reported an elevated rate of alexithymia in individuals who have experienced CSA (e.g., Hund & Espelage, 2005; Mazzeo & Espelage, 2002; Scher & Twaite, 1999). Deficits in the recognition and generation of emotional expressions (Camras et al., 1988) and the ability to label one's own feelings (Berenbaum, 1996) are prominent in sexually abused populations relative to non-sexually abused controls.

According to the clinical literature, dissociation may also be a common response to traumatic experiences (e.g., Banyard, Williams, & Siegel, 2001; Morgan et al., 2001) and may interfere with memory integration and elaboration (Ehlers & Clark, 2000; Harvey & Bryant, 1999; Murray, Ehlers, & Mayou, 2002). Kisiel and Lyons (2001) evaluated dissociative tendencies in a sample of 114 children and adolescents with known histories of abuse (sexual, physical) and neglect. They found that sexual abuse was associated with the highest levels of dissociation relative to other abuse groups and non-abuse controls. It is possible that the lack of psychological integration characteristic of dissociation would result in disintegrated memories. For example, some researchers argue that with increased levels of dissociation, elements of traumatic events may only be partially encoded (e.g., shallow processing), especially when "disconnected" from the event (Berliner et al., 2003). Other research, however, has failed to find a relationship between traumatic events and dissociative amnesia (e.g., Geraerts et al., 2007).

Both alexithymic and dissociative tendencies appear to be related to susceptibility to memory distortion (e.g., Candel, Merckelbach, & Kuijpers, 2003; Porter, Birt, Yuille, & Lehman, 2000; Zoellner, Foa, Brigidi, & Przeworski, 2000). In light of this, it would be expected that memory quality, vividness, coherence, and relevance would be negatively related to higher levels of these factors. However, some studies have found no relation between dissociation and traumatic memory deficits (Berliner et al., 2003). No research has yet compared the roles of alexithymia and dissociation in memory for sexually and non-sexually traumatic experiences.

THE CURRENT STUDY

The current study was intended to provide a comprehensive within-subjects investigation of memory for sexual trauma, non-sexual trauma, and positive emotional events in a clinical sample. We predicted, contrary to the brief survey findings of Koss et al. (1996), that narratives concerning sexual victimisation would not evidence impairment relative to other types of emotional experiences. Rather, we hypothesised that the recollection of sexually traumatic events may be enhanced relative to other emotional experiences. However, this predicted pattern could be mediated by the age at the time of the traumatic experience, level of traumatic stress, alexithymia, and dissociation.

METHOD

Participants

The sample was 44 adult females who had been referred for counselling at a sexual assault centre or psychological agency in eastern Canada. All referred clients had a documented history of sexual victimisation. Participants responded to advertisements for a memory study about emotional events (sexual trauma, non-sexual trauma, positive event) that were posted at the agency offices. The mean age of the participants was 30.1 years ($SD = 8.9$; range 18–52).

Measures

Written narratives. Participants were provided with a questionnaire inquiring about a sexually traumatic experience, a non-sexually traumatic experience, and a positive emotional experience. Participants were asked to select traumatic and positive events in the same general age range (e.g., childhood, adolescence, adulthood) as the sexually traumatic experience. For each event type (counterbalanced), participants were asked to choose a specific event (rather than a series of events) and write out everything they could remember about the incident in as much detail as possible. They were also instructed not to go back in the questionnaire after they had completed a particular section.

All women in the sample reported either an incident of CSA (43.2%) or an adult sexual assault (56.8%).[1] The reported non-sexual traumas were: death of a loved one (27.3%), criminal victimisation (22.7%), accident/injury (20.5%), relationship related (9.1%), medical condition (9.1%), or other (6.8%). Two women did not provide the non-sexual trauma description. The positive events included: relationship related (25%), celebration/graduation (22.7%), other (22.7%), unexpected gift (13.6%), or vacation (9.1%). Three women did not provide the positive event description.

Impact of Event Scale (IES). The IES (Horowitz, Wilner, & Alvarez, 1979) is a 15-item self-report questionnaire involves rating the frequency of various cognitive experiences in relation to a traumatic event (e.g., I tried not to think about it; any reminder brought back feelings about it) on a scale marked 0 (not at all), 1 (rarely), 3 (sometimes), and 5 (often). The IES contains two subscales measuring intrusion in daily life, and avoidance of memories and stimuli associated with the event. A total score is generated by combining the subscale scores, and provides an assessment of the overall level of impact of an event. This scale was administered with respect to sexual trauma (Cronbach's $\alpha = .91$), non-sexual trauma (Cronbach's $\alpha = .89$), and positive events (Cronbach's $\alpha = .84$). This scale has been extensively used with trauma victims (Foa & Rothbaum, 1998; Peace & Porter, 2004), and is a reliable measure of post-traumatic impact (e.g., Briere, 1997; Carlson, 1997).

Memory Assessment Procedure (MAP). The MAP (Porter, Yuille, & Lehman, 1999) was used as an assessment tool to examine the qualitative aspects of memory reports (e.g., see Porter & Birt, 2001). This procedure evaluates a variety of presentation-specific characteristics, such as coherence, amount of detail, and emotional components, rated by coders. An inter-rater reliability check was conducted by having a second rater (naïve to the hypothesis of the study and trained on MAP criteria) recode 20% of the memories elicited in the study. The coding had high inter-rater reliability for each of sexual trauma, non-sexual trauma, and positive

[1] All events were classified as child (0–13) or adult (14+) based on the legal age of consent to sexual activity in Canada.

experiences, with all correlations ranging from .86 to .97 (all $ps < .001$) and no significant mean differences on any variables ($ps > .05$).

The MAP also measures phenomenological (completed by participant) characteristics of memory, as completed in the Emotional Memory Survey (EMS). The EMS required the completion of 15 items pertaining to the participant's view of her memory features. The EMS uses a 7-point Likert scale on some questions (e.g., indicate how often you have thought about the event; indicate how vivid your memory is for the event), and YES/NO responses on others (e.g., was there ever a period of time where you could not remember the event?). This survey also asked participants to indicate sensory and emotional experiences associated with the event.

20-Item Toronto Alexithymia Scale (TAS-20). The TAS-20 (Cronbach's $\alpha = .85$; Bagby, Parker, & Taylor, 1994; Bagby, Taylor, & Parker, 1994) was used to examine the extent to which participants have deficits in processing and regulating emotions, including the ability to identify one's own emotions. This is a 20-item self-report questionnaire that describes a range of statements concerning emotions. Participants rate how similar the statement is to their own experiences, on a scale from 1 (strongly disagree) to 5 (strongly agree).

Dissociative Experiences Scale (DES). The DES (Cronbach's $\alpha = .95$; Bernstein & Putnam, 1986) is a 28-item self-administered questionnaire that describes a range of common dissociative experiences (e.g., being unaware of other events when absorbed in watching a movie) to severe indications of dissociation (e.g., not recognising family members and friends). Participants rated how often the experiences described happen to them (in terms of a percentage from 0% to 100%; increments of 10%). A single score is calculated, with higher scores being related to higher degrees of dissociative tendencies. The DES has been demonstrated to show good reliability, internal consistency, and construct validity in this regard (Carlson & Putnam, 1993).

Research design

This study had a mixed multivariate design with memory type (sexual trauma, non-sexual trauma, positive) as the main within-subjects variable and event age category as the between-subjects factor within each memory type. Counterbalancing was entered into each statistical analysis and no significant order effects were found (all $ps > .05$).

Procedure

After reviewing the posted ad, potential participants informed their counsellor of their interest in participating. After reviewing and signing the informed consent form, participants received a Memory Survey Booklet consisting of several memory report forms and questionnaires. Instructions were given verbally and in writing to each participant, to complete the entire packet within a week of receipt, preferably in a single sitting. Due to the sensitive nature of the experiences being recalled, participants completed the packets on their own time, similar to previous studies using a mail survey format (e.g., Koss et al., 1996).

A Written Narrative Memory Report form was included for each type of event, with the order of presentation counterbalanced in each survey package. Participants provided a written description of a sexually traumatic memory (STM), a non-sexually traumatic memory (NSTM), and a positive emotional memory (PM). The written instructions have been used in previous research on traumatic memories (Peace & Porter, 2004; Porter & Birt, 2001), and were slightly modified for each memory type here. After providing each narrative, participants answered questions on the IES and EMS regarding a particular event. After describing the STM, NSTM, and PM, the TAS-20 and DES were administered.

RESULTS

Emotional memory characteristics

To investigate possible differences in memory characteristics as a function of event type, a repeated measures MANOVA was conducted. Memory type was the within-subjects independent variable and subjective memory characteristics (EMS)[2] were the dependent measures. This analysis revealed an overall effect of memory

[2] Subjective characteristics included anxiety/stress, degree of intoxication, talking/thinking about event, memory vividness and quality, sensory components, turning off emotions, becoming emotional, detachment, and emotional intensity.

type, $F(22, 136) = 8.23$, $p < .001$. Follow-up ANOVAs indicated differences on several self-reported memory characteristics including vividness of memory, $F(2, 78) = 7.41$, $p < .001$, sensory components, $F(2, 78) = 10.96$, $p < .001$, and emotional intensity, $F(2, 78) = 22.85$, $p < .001$ (see Table 1). For each of these features, sexually traumatic events were rated higher than the other memory types.

Participants also were asked to rate (for each memory type) whether there was "ever a period of time when you did not remember the event even if you had tried" (repression). Overall, 9 (20.5%) sexual traumas were associated with claims of repression relative to 2 (4.8%) of non-sexual traumas and 0 positive experiences. A non-parametric analysis was used to rank order responses, and revealed that self-reports of repression were significantly different, Kendall's $W = .17$, $\chi^2 = 13.40$, $p < .01$. Self-reported attempts to "forget" the event ranged from 43.2% for sexual traumas, 11.9% for non-sexual traumas, to 2.4% for positive events. Self-reported "forgetting" of sexual trauma was significantly higher than both non-sexual and positive event ratings, Kendall's $W = .28$, $\chi^2 = 22.57$, $p < .001$.

An additional MANOVA was conducted using for the MAP criteria[3] as the dependent variables across the memory types (see Table 1). The MANOVA revealed a significant main effect of memory type, $F(16, 24) = 2.86$, $p < .01$. Sexually traumatic experiences were associated with the greatest amount of detail, $F(2, 78) = 29.74$, $p < .001$, more emotional components, $F(2, 78) = 9.98$, $p < .001$, more time and place details, $F(2, 78) = 7.75$, $p \leq .001$, more reasons for lack of memory, $F(2, 78) = 10.15$, $p < .001$, and highest word counts, $F(2, 78) = 28.74$, $p < .001$ (see Table 1).

Memory characteristics as a function of age of occurrence

The specific mean age at the time of sexual trauma was 17.16 ($SD = 9.88$; range 3–51). The mean age for CSA was 8.83 ($SD = 8.46$) and 22.18 ($SD = 7.58$) for sexual assault. The mean age of occurrence for non-sexually traumatic events was 19.13 ($SD = 9.48$; range 3.5–42). Finally, positive emotional events occurred around age 20.81 ($SD = 10.29$; range 4.5–51). There is no significant difference between the mean ages for each memory type, $F(2, 74) = 2.88$, $p > .05$.

To address whether memory characteristics differed for CSA and adult sexual assault experiences, a MANOVA was conducted with age category as the between-subjects factor and memory characteristics as the dependent measures. The analysis revealed no overall main effect of age, $F(28, 15) = 1.21$, $p > .05$. However, univariate analyses revealed that CSA was associated with more claims of repression, $F(1, 42) = 10.22$, $p < .01$, and less coherent memory reports, $F(1, 42) = 5.34$, $p < .05$. A similar analysis was used for age comparisons within non-sexually traumatic experiences, and an effect of age approached significance, $F(28, 13) = 2.16$, $p = .07$. Specifically, childhood traumas were less vivid, $F(1, 40) = 4.05$, $p = .05$, and associated with periods of forgetting, $F(1, 40) = 14.82$, $p < .001$; associated with more claims of repression, $F(1, 40) = 4.44$, $p < .05$; with memory problems, $F(1, 40) = 14.82$, $p < .001$; and providing reasons for lack of memory, $F(1, 40) = 4.44$, $p < .05$. A multivariate analysis of differences across age ranges for positive memories also approached significance, $F(27, 12) = 2.45$, $p = .06$. Follow-up analyses indicated that positive childhood experiences were rated as lower in: emotional intensity, $F(1, 38) = 4.46$, $p < .05$, levels of becoming emotional, $F(1, 38) = 5.84$, $p < .05$, coherence, $F(1, 38) = 5.89$, $p < .05$, and degree of intoxication, $F(1, 38) = 4.31$, $p < .05$, relative to positive adult experiences. In addition, positive events in childhood contained more emotional details about other people relative to narratives of positive adult experiences, $F(1, 38) = 7.12$, $p < .05$.

Psychological impact and remembering

The mean IES scores for each event type was: STM 55.66 ($SD = 14.26$), NSTM 41.55 ($SD = 14.10$), and PM 19.46 ($SD = 9.44$). Sexual traumas were also associated with the highest levels of intrusion ($M = 26.77$, $SD = 7.24$) and avoidance ($M = 28.89$, $SD = 8.02$), relative to non-sexual traumas ($M = 21.93$, $SD = 7.67$ and $M = 19.62$, $SD = 7.40$, respectively) and positive experiences ($M = 15.15$, $SD = 7.14$, and $M = 4.32$, $SD = 3.92$). A repeated measures MANOVA was conducted on levels of traumatic stress as a function of

[3] Objective characteristics included amount of detail, time and place details, emotional components, relevance, coherence, reasons for lack of memory, and word count.

TABLE 1
Subjective and objective memory characteristics

Memory characteristics	*STM*	*NSTM*	*PM*
Subjective			
Anxiety/stress***	6.48(0.85)	$5.90(1.22)_b$	$4.08(1.99)_c$
Degree of intoxication	$1.85(1.67)_a$	$1.40(1.10)_a$	$1.75(1.24)_a$
Talked about event***	$3.7(1.68)_a$	$5.05(1.54)_b$	$5.20(1.32)_b$
Thought about event	$6.08(1.19)_a$	$5.75(1.10)_{a,b}$	$5.48(1.24)_b$
Vividness of memory***	$6.25(1.13)_a$	$5.45(1.30)_b$	$5.20(1.14)_b$
Quality of memory	$5.45(1.47)_a$	$5.18(1.45)_a$	$5.08(1.21)_a$
Sensory components***	$3.38(0.93)_a$	$2.45(0.78)_b$	$2.55(1.08)_b$
"Turned off" emotions***	$5.28(1.55)_a$	$3.95(1.50)_b$	$2.03(1.12)_c$
Becoming emotional***	$6.30(0.85)_a$	$5.43(1.38)_b$	$4.53(1.45)_c$
Detachment***	$5.10(1.48)_a$	$3.70(1.76)_b$	$1.55(0.99)_c$
Emotional intensity***	$6.68(0.53)_a$	$6.03(1.00)_b$	$5.45(0.99)_c$
Objective			
Amount of detail***	$316.68(238.68)_a$	$159.10(75.81)_b$	$103.98(51.81)_c$
Emotional details(self)***	$4.58(5.62)_a$	$1.90(1.98)_b$	$1.50(1.81)_b$
Emotional details(others)	$1.03(1.58)_a$	$0.83(1.28)_{a,b}$	$0.50(1.45)_b$
Time and place details***	$13.58(11.79)_a$	$9.18(7.32)_b$	$6.53(5.87)_b$
Relevance	$5.85(1.05)_a$	$6.05(0.96)_a$	$5.73(0.93)_a$
Coherence	$5.93(1.12)_{a,b,c}$	$6.13(0.88)_{a,b}$	$5.73(1.01)_{a,c}$
Lack of memory***	$0.35(0.53)_a$	$0.05(0.22)_b$	$0.03(0.13)_b$
Word Count***	$591.63(453.04)_a$	$291.05(138.56)_b$	$194.75(101.05)_c$

Means (and standard deviations) for subjective (EMS) and objective (MAP) memory characteristics for sexual (STM) and non-sexual (NSTM) trauma and positive (PM) experiences. Means in the same row that do not share subscripts differ at a minimum of $p < .05$ in the Fisher LSD comparison.
**p* <.05. ***p* <.01. ****p* ≤.001.

memory type, and significant mean differences were revealed. Sexual traumas contained the highest mean total IES rating relative to non-sexual traumas and positive experiences, $F(2, 78) = 138.47$, $p < .0001$. Pairwise comparisons indicated that non-sexual and positive experiences also differed on the total level of impact of the event, $t(39) = 9.19$, $p < .0001$. Sexual traumas were also associated with the highest mean level of intrusive, $F(2, 78) = 49.10$, $p < .0001$, and avoidant symptomatology, $F(2, 78) = 199.61$, $p < .0001$. Follow-up analyses indicated that non-sexual traumas and positive experiences differed significantly on their mean level of intrusion $t(39) = 4.9$, $p < .0001$, and avoidance, $t(39) = 11.98$, $p < .0001$.

Correlational analyses also were conducted to assess the association between level of impact and memory characteristics (see Table 2).[4] More severe sexual traumas were associated with becoming more emotional and experiencing negative emotions when discussing the event. Higher IES scores were also associated with higher levels of alexithymia, $r(44) = .51$, $p < .001$. There were no associations between level of impact and dissociation or alexithymia for either non-sexual traumas or positive events. For non-sexual traumas, higher IES total scores were associated with more thoughts, vividness, and emotionality surrounding the event, but were unrelated to any objective memory characteristics. Positive events with a higher "impact" were positively correlated with more anxiety/stress and thoughts about the event.

The role of alexithymia and dissociation

The mean alexithymia score (TAS) was 56.27 ($SD = 12.26$; range 26–80) and the mean DES score was 20.22 ($SD = 10.99$; range 5–50). There was a positive association between levels of dissociation and alexithymia, $r(44) = .62$, $p < .001$, suggesting that these two constructs have overlapping features in victimised populations. Both variables were correlated with a number of self-reported and objective features of both traumatic and non-traumatic events (see Table 2 for

[4] The Bonferroni correction was applied to this correlational analysis. To avoid spurious results, the corrected alpha level was set at $\alpha = .002$.

TABLE 2
Memory characteristics, event impact, dissociation, and alexithymia

Memory characteristics	*IES*	*DES*	*TAS-20*
Sexual trauma (STM)			
IES total score	—	.41	.51*
DES total score	.41	—	.62
TAS-20 total score	.51*	.62*	—
Memory quality	.31	−.52*	−.22
Turned off emotions	.26	.69*	.47*
Becoming emotional	.50*	.39	.29
Feeling detached	.24	.65	.59
Negative feelings when discussing	.54*	.29	.13
Repression claims	−.14	.57*	.27
Non-sexual trauma (NSTM)			
Memory vividness	.46*	−.37	−.21
Thoughts about event	.46*	.10	.05
Becoming emotional	.71*	−.02	.12
Negative feelings when discussing	.48*	.27	.14
Positive events (PM)			
Age at time of event	−.02	−.33	−.47*
Anxiety/stress	.50*	−.34	−.20
Thoughts about event	.46*	−.05	.12

Characteristics of memories (by type) significantly correlated with levels of event impact (IES), dissociation (DES,) and alexithymia (TAS-20).

*$p \leq .002$ (as per Bonferroni correction).

correlations). Notably, both DES and TAS-20 scores were associated with characteristics of sexually traumatic experiences more so than with non-sexual traumatic or positive events. Dissociation was related to emotional deficits, claims of repression, memory problems, and a lower quality of memory. However, levels of alexithymia were most strongly associated with levels of stress and emotional separation (e.g., "turned off" emotions, detachment). In addition, higher levels of alexithymia were related to a younger age at which the experience occurred (i.e., childhood) for positive memories only.

DISCUSSION

While clinical and scientific interest in memory for trauma is enormous (e.g., McNally, 2003), important issues remain unresolved. In particular, there is a long-standing notion that memory for trauma—in particular, sexual trauma—is typically impaired or unreliable. There are two very different lines of thought hypothesising that traumatic memories may not persist over time. The first emphasises that trauma actively impairs memories leading to fractured recollections. According to Spiegel (1997), traumatic events are unlike other types of events in that they are resistant to retrieval in memory. The second argues that traumatic memories simply are not unique relative to other memories and show a natural deterioration over time, not because of the trauma but because of ordinary forgetting and a host of suggestive influences or misinformation (for a review see Laney & Loftus, 2005). However, recent studies suggest that trauma generally is not associated with impairment or ordinary forgetting, and rather may even facilitate the qualities and reliability of memory (e.g., Porter & Peace, in press).

Our findings partially supported our hypothesis that memories for sexual victimisation would not be impaired relative to other types of emotional experiences. Memories for sexual trauma contained the greatest amount of detail, more emotional components, a higher degree of vividness, and more sensory information. Thus, both subjectively and objectively, the sexual memories had endured in quality years or decades after the events. On the other hand, sexually traumatic memories concurrently were associated with the highest rates of self-reported memory problems (43.2%) and claims of repression (20.5%), relative to nonsexual traumas (11.9% and 4.8%, respectively) and positive events (2.4% and 0%). There are several possible explanations for these findings. A simple explanation is that estimates of memory problems and repression were inflated due to semantic misinterpretations of questions. For example, participants may have reported experiencing memory problems with respect to active attempts not to remember (suppression), not consciously thinking about the event due to avoidance or detachment, or an inability to forget. Further, because of the popularity of the repression concept in society, they may have responded in a manner that they believed would be expected. In addition, all women in the sample were seeking counselling to deal with sexual victimisation, which makes them unique in several ways. A recent study by Geraerts et al. (2006) suggests that participants reporting recovered memories of CSA may overestimate their prior forgetting of the abuse. Further, it is possible that memory, repression, and fragmented recall would have been discussed in this therapeutic context, in conjunction with the use of memory techniques directed at eliciting details of the sexual trauma. Previous research has found that such techniques may lead to inflated self-reports of memory problems relative to genuine recall abilities. For example, Read and Lindsay (2000) found that following retrieval activities targeted at improving recall of autobiographical events, participants reported higher levels of previous memory problems related to that event. Further, in most cases "memory problems" were manifested here by problems with forgetting (in terms of the intrusive memories indicated by the IES) rather than remembering. Overall, memory reports for sexual trauma were well retained and not impaired as previous research has suggested.

We also predicted that the qualities of traumatic memories would be affected by the age when the event occurred. However, there were few differences in memories for childhood versus adulthood sexual trauma. CSA was associated with less coherent memory narratives and more claims of prior forgetting (or repression) relative to adult sexual assault experiences. It is possible that CSA (especially incidents from early childhood) may have been processed or encoded less coherently in the first place. Further, CSA often involves repeated victimisations over an extended period. Although women in this sample were asked to report on their memory for a specific incident of abuse/assault, it is possible that CSA memories were less coherent because details from other abusive experiences had merged with the incident being recalled. This would tend to make the memory report appear less logical and organised, as details within a "trauma script" for abuse may not apply to all incidents. Additionally, claims of repression and memory problems were more frequent for early childhood experiences regardless of trauma type (sexual or non-sexual). Geraerts et al. (2006) found that persons reporting recovered memories of CSA (compared to a CSA group with continuous memory for the abuse and a control group) are more likely to forget prior rememberings of autobiographical events. That is, while they may believe they have forgotten an event all along, it has been recalled previously. Thus, increased reports of repression in CSA cases may be influenced not only by cultural beliefs and discussion in therapy but also by inaccurate metamemory. Additionally, frequent memory problems suggest that self-reported memory difficulties are not due to the nature of sexual trauma, but that younger children have more difficulty in recalling traumatic experiences (in general) due to phenomena such as infantile amnesia and normal forgetting (e.g., Pezdek & Taylor, 2002). Further, participants may perceive that they have memory difficulties due to the reduced availability of childhood traumas in memory relative to more recent events. For example, participants sometimes report that they have problems recalling an event when the memory does not readily come to mind or they have to engage in more extensive cognitive effort to remember (McNally, 2003; Read & Lindsay, 2000).

We also examined the relation between level of traumatic stress and memory quality. Our findings indicated that higher levels of traumatic stress were associated with enhanced recall. Sexual traumas with heightened levels of traumatic stress were associated with greater vividness, sensory components, details, and length, relative to other emotional experiences. Further, increased stress was unrelated to claims of repression or memory problems in sexual traumas. This supports previous research conclusions that traumatic impact facilitates memory (e.g., Alexander et al., 2005; Porter & Birt, 2001). Here, severe levels of impact did not impair memories for traumatic events in any way.

The final aim of this study was to evaluate the role of alexithymia and dissociation in recollections for sexually traumatic events. Results indicated that higher levels of alexithymia and dissociation were associated with pathological emotional experiences (detachment) and narrative deficiencies across all memory types. Difficulties associated with alexithymia including identifying and describing feelings have been linked to cognitive-affective deficits in assimilating the event in memory (Páez, Velasco, & González, 1999). Further, dissociation and alexithymia were most frequently associated with variations (i.e., changes in affect, less introspective memory reports) in the recall of sexual traumas. High levels of dissociation were correlated with emotional deficits, claims of repression, memory problems, and a lower quality of memory. This finding is unsurprising given the nature of dissociation and its association with detached modes of coping (e.g., Nash, Tulsey, Sexton, Harralson, & Lambert, 1993) and memory distortion (e.g., Hyman & Billings, 1998; Porter et al., 2000). Conversely, alexithymia was associated with increased stress, and a greater degree of emotional separation from the event (e.g., "turned off" feelings, detachment). These results support previously established associations between high levels of alexithymia and sexual trauma (e.g., Guttman & Laporte, 2002), and increased scores of emotional inhibition on measures of affect (e.g., Páez et al., 1999).

Given the common assumption that it is severe trauma that can produce dissociation, the results of the current study may seem paradoxical, in that memories for severe trauma were found to be remarkably detailed while dissociation was associated with memory impairment. The results of Geraerts et al. (2006) suggest that narrative deficiencies such as claims of repression, memory problems, emotional detachment, and perceived quality of the memory may be misinterpretations of metamemory for a traumatic memory that is actually quite detailed in nature. Thus, both superior objective measures of traumatic memories and subjective narrative deficiencies may exist without conflict.

Some limitations of the current research should be noted. Like some previous studies that have supported the trauma superiority argument, participants in this study have likely spent some amount of time recalling their victimisation during therapy sessions. Similarly, Nazi concentration camp survivors and CSA victims in previous studies have recounted their victimisations in numerous legal trials (Alexander et al., 2005; Wagenaar & Groeneweg, 1990). Although the experience of recalling victimisation in therapy or on the witness stand may not be an unusual experience for victims of sexual abuse, it should be noted that the current results may not generalise to victims who are not made to recollect their trauma repeatedly. Given the nature of therapeutic interventions, differential attention is given to memories of sexual abuse, which may affect the quality of these memories relative to other traumatic or positive autobiographical events and may be reflected in the results of this study. Additionally, like most research on trauma and memory, a limitation is that we did not have access to ground truth, and focused exclusively on the self-reported narratives to assess memory qualities. As such, we can comment only on the features of the memories but not on their reliability.

Conclusion

Collectively, the results of the present study demonstrate that contrary to previous research, memories for sexual trauma were not impaired or fragmented. In contrast, in some ways these memories were "superior" to other emotional memories regardless of the belief of participants, especially in CSA cases, that their memory was impaired. Further, we found that high levels of traumatic impact did not cause subsequent memory deficits. Individual difference factors such as dissociation and alexithymia appeared to influence self-reported assessments about memory or emotional problems, but were generally unrelated to objectively rated memory characteristics. In general, we found little evidence for the traumatic memory argument and considerable evidence that sexual trauma is remembered all too well years after the experience.

Manuscript received 31 October 2006
Manuscript accepted 20 March 2007
First published online 17 May 2007

REFERENCES

Alexander, K. W., Quas, J. A., Goodman, G. S., Ghetti, S., Edelstein, R. S., Redlich, A. D., et al. (2005). Traumatic impact predicts long-term memory for documented child sexual abuse. *Psychological Science, 16*, 33–40.

Bagby, R. M., Parker, J. D. A., & Taylor, G. J. (1994). The twenty-item Toronto Alexithymia Scale-I: Item selection and cross-validation of the factor structure. *Journal of Psychosomatic Research, 38*, 23–32.

Bagby, R. M., Taylor, G. J., & Parker, J. D. A. (1994). The twenty-item Toronto Alexithymia Scale-II: Convergent, discriminant and concurrent validity. *Journal of Psychosomatic Research, 38*, 33–40.

Banyard, V. L., Williams, L. M., & Siegel, J. A. (2001). Understanding links among childhood trauma, dissociation, and women's mental health. *American Journal of Orthopsychiatry, 71*, 311–321.

Berenbaum, H. (1996). Childhood abuse, alexithymia and personality disorder. *Journal of Psychosomatic Research, 41*, 585–595.

Berliner, L., Hyman, I., Thomas, A., & Fitzgerald, M. (2003). Children's memory for trauma and positive experiences. *Journal of Traumatic Stress, 16*, 229–236.

Bernstein, E. M., & Putnam, F. W. (1986). Development, reliability, and validity of a dissociation scale. *Journal of Nervous and Mental Disease, 174*, 727–735.

Berntsen, D. (2001). Involuntary memories of emotional events: Do memories of traumas and extremely happy events differ? *Applied Cognitive Psychology, 15*, 135–158.

Berntsen, D., Willert, M., & Rubin, D. C. (2003). Splintered memories or vivid landmarks? Qualities and organization of traumatic memories with and without PTSD. *Applied Cognitive Psychology, 17*, 675–693.

Brewin, C. R. (2001). Memory processes in posttraumatic stress disorder. *International Review of Psychiatry, 13*, 159–163.

Brewin, C. R., Dalgleish, T., & Joseph, S. (1996). A dual representation theory of Posttraumatic Stress Disorder. *Psychological Review, 103*, 670–686.

Briere, J. (1997). *Psychological assessment of adult posttraumatic states.* Washington, DC: American Psychological Association.

Byrne, C. A., Hyman, I. E., & Scott, K. L. (2001). Comparisons of memories for traumatic events and other experiences. *Applied Cognitive Psychology, 15*, S119–S133.

Camras, L. A., Ribordy, S., Hill, J., Martino, S., Spaccarelli, S., & Stefani, R. (1988). Recognition and posing of emotional expressions by abused children and their mothers. *Developmental Psychology, 24*, 776–781.

Candel, I., Merckelbach, H., & Kuijpers, M. (2003). Dissociative experiences are related to commissions in emotional memory. *Behaviour Research and Therapy, 41*, 719–725.

Carlson, E. B. (1997). *Trauma assessments: A clinician's guide.* New York: Guilford Press.

Carlson, E. B., & Putnam, F. W. (1993). An update on the Dissociative Experiences Scale. *Dissociation, 6*, 16–24.

Ehlers, A., & Clark, D. M. (2000). A cognitive model of posttraumatic stress disorder. *Behaviour Research and Therapy, 38*, 319–345.

Foa, E. B., Molnar, C., & Cashman, L. (1995). Change in rape narratives during exposure therapy for Posttraumatic Stress Disorder. *Journal of Traumatic Stress, 8*, 675–690.

Foa, E. B., & Rothbaum, B. O. (1998). *Treating the trauma of rape: Cognitive-behavioral therapy for PTSD.* New York: Guilford Press.

Geraerts, E., Arnold, M. M., Lindsay, D. S., Merckelbach, H., Jelicic, M., & Hauer, B. (2006). Forgetting of prior remembering in persons reporting recovered memories of childhood sexual abuse. *Psychological Science, 17*, 1002–1008.

Geraerts, E., Kozarić-Kovačić, D., Merckelbach, H., Peraica, T., Jelicic, M., & Candel, I. (2007). Traumatic memories of war veterans: Not so special after all. *Consciousness and Cognition, 16*, 170–177.

Griesel, D., Cooper, B. S., Hernandez, A. R., & Yuille, J. C. (2005, June). Quality of recall in sex trade workers' memories of sexual violence: A pilot study. In K. A. Peace (Chair), *Memory and psychology in forensic contexts.* Symposium conducted at the meeting of the Canadian Psychological Association, Montreal, Quebec, Canada.

Guttman, H., & Laporte, L. (2002). Alexithymia, empathy, and psychological symptoms in a family context. *Comprehensive Psychiatry, 43*, 448–455.

Halligan, S. L., Michael, T., Clark, D. M., & Ehlers, A. (2003). Posttraumatic stress disorder following assault: The role of cognitive processing, trauma memory, and appraisals. *Journal of Consulting and Clinical Psychology, 71*, 419–431.

Hanson, R. F., Saunders, B., Kilpatrick, D., Resnick, H., Crouch, J. A., & Duncan, R. (2001). Impact of childhood rape and aggravated assault on adult mental health. *American Journal of Orthopsychiatry, 71*, 108–119.

Harvey, A. G., & Bryant, R. A. (1999). A qualitative investigation of the organization of traumatic memories. *British Journal of Clinical Psychology, 38*, 401–405.

Horowitz, M. J., Wilner, N., & Alvarez, W. (1979). Impact of Event Scale: A measure of subjective stress. *Psychosomatic Medicine, 41*, 209–218.

Hund, A. R., & Espelage, D. L. (2005). Childhood sexual abuse, disordered eating, alexithymia, and general distress: A mediation model. *Journal of Counseling Psychology, 52*, 559–573.

Hyman, I. E., & Billings, F. J. (1998). Individual differences and the creation of false childhood memories. *Memory, 6*, 1–20.

Hyman, I. E., & Byrne, C. A. (1999, July). *Differences between trauma memories and memories of other experiences.* Paper presented at the meeting of SARMAC: Society for Applied Research in Memory and Cognition, Boulder, CO.

Kenny, M. (1998). The proof is in the passion: Emotion as an index of veridical memory. In J. de Rivera & T. R. Sarbin (Eds.), *Believed-in imaginings: The narrative construction of reality* (pp. 269–293). Washington, DC: APA.

Kisiel, C. L., & Lyons, J. S. (2001). Dissociation as a mediator of psychopathology among sexually abused children and adolescents. *American Journal of Psychiatry, 158*, 1034–1039.

Koss, M. P., Figueredo, A. J., Bell, I., Tharan, M., & Tromp, S. (1996). Traumatic memory characteristics: A cross-validated mediational model of response to rape among employed women. *Journal of Abnormal Psychology, 105*, 421–432.

Koss, M. P., Figueredo, A. J., Bell, I., Tharan, M., & Tromp, S. (1999). Traumatic memory characteristics: A cross-validated mediational model of response to rape among employed women. In L. M. Williams & V. L. Banyard (Eds.), *Trauma & memory* (pp. 273–290). Thousand Oaks, CA: Sage Publications.

Laney, C., & Loftus, E. F. (2005). Traumatic memories are not necessarily accurate memories. *Canadian Journal of Psychiatry, 50*, 823–828.

Lumley, M. A., Gustavson, B. J., Partridge, R. T., & Labouvie-Vief, G. (2005). Assessing alexithymia and related emotional ability constructs using multiple methods: Interrelationships among measures. *Emotion, 5*, 329–342.

Mazzeo, S. E., & Espelage, D. L. (2002). Association between childhood physical and emotional abuse and disordered eating behaviors in female undergraduates: An investigation of the mediating role of alexithymia and depression. *Journal of Counseling Psychology, 49*, 86–100.

McNally, R. J. (2003). *Remembering trauma.* Cambridge, MA: Harvard University Press.

Merckelbach, H., Dekkers, T., Wessel, I., & Roefs, A. (2003). Amnesia, flashbacks, nightmares, and dissociation in aging concentration camp survivors. *Behaviour Research and Therapy, 41*, 351–360.

Morgan, C. A. III., Hazlett, G., Wang, S., Richardson, E. G., Schnurr, P., & Southwick, S. M. (2001). Symptoms of dissociation in humans experiencing acute, uncontrollable stress: A prospective investigation *American Journal of Psychiatry, 158*, 1239–1247.

Murray, J., Ehlers, A., & Mayou, R. A. (2002). Dissociation and posttraumatic stress disorder: Two prospective studies of motor vehicle accident survivors. *British Journal of Psychiatry, 180*, 363–368.

Nadel, L., & Jacobs, W. J. (1998). Traumatic memory is special. *Current Directions in Psychological Science, 7*, 154–157.

Nash, M. R., Tulsey, T. L., Sexton, M. C., Harralson, T. L., & Lambert, W. (1993). Long-term sequelae of childhood sexual abuse: Perceived family environment, psychopathology, and dissociation. *Journal of Consulting and Clinical Psychology, 61*, 276–283.

Ofshe, R., & Watters, E. (1994). *Making monsters: False memories, psychotherapy, and sexual hysteria.* New York: Scribner's.

Páez, D., Velasco, C., & González, J. L. (1999). Expressive writing and the role of alexithymia as a dispositional deficit in self-disclosure and psychological health. *Journal of Personality and Social Psychology, 77*, 630–641.

Peace, K. A., & Porter, S. (2004). A longitudinal investigation of the reliability of memories for trauma and other emotional experiences. *Applied Cognitive Psychology, 18*, 1143–1159.

Pezdek, K., & Taylor, J. (2002). Memory for traumatic events in children and adults. In M. L. Eisen, J. A. Quas, & G. S. Goodman (Eds.), *Memory and suggestibility in the forensic interview* (pp. 165–183). Mahwah, NJ: Lawrence Erlbaum Associates Inc.

Porter, S., & Birt, A. R. (2001). Is traumatic memory special? A comparison of traumatic memory characteristics with memory for other emotional life experiences. *Applied Cognitive Psychology, 15*, 1–17.

Porter, S., Birt, A. R., Yuille, J. C., & Lehman, D. R. (2000). Negotiating false memories: Interviewer and rememberer characteristics relate to memory distortion. *Psychological Science, 11*, 507–510.

Porter, S., & Peace, K. A. (in press). The scars of memory: A prospective, longitudinal investigation of the consistency of traumatic memories in adulthood. *Psychological Science.*

Porter, S., Yuille, J. C., & Lehman, D. R. (1999). The nature of real, implanted, and fabricated memories for emotional childhood events: Implications for the recovered memory debate. *Law and Human Behavior, 23*, 517–537.

Read, J. D., & Lindsay, D. S. (2000). "Amnesia" for summer camps and high school graduation: Memory work increases reports of prior periods of remembering less. *Journal of Traumatic Stress, 13*, 129–147.

Rind, B., Tromovitch, R., & Bauserman, R. (1998). A meta-analytic examination of assumed properties of child sexual abuse using college samples. *Psychological Bulletin, 124*, 22–53.

Roemer, L., Litz, B. T., Orsillo, S. M., Ehlich, P., & Friedman, M. (1998). Increases in retrospective accounts of war-zone exposure over time: The role of PTSD symptom severity. *Journal of Traumatic Stress, 11*, 597–607.

Rubin, D. C., Feldman, M. E., & Beckham, J. C. (2004). Reliving, emotions, and fragmentation in the autobiographical memories of veterans diagnosed with PTSD. *Applied Cognitive Psychology, 18*, 17–35.

Schelach, L., & Nachson, I. (2001). Memory of Auschwitz survivors. *Applied Cognitive Psychology, 15*, 119–132.

Scher, D., & Twaite, J. A. (1999). The relationship between child sexual abuse and alexithymic symptoms in a population of recovering adult substance abusers. *Journal of Child Sexual Abuse, 8*, 25–40.

Schiraldi, G. R. (2000). *The post-traumatic stress disorder sourcebook: A guide to healing, recovery, and growth.* Los Angeles: Lowell House.

Spiegel, D. (1997). Trauma, dissociation, and memory. *Annals of the New York Academy of Science, 821*, 225–237.

Taylor, G. J. (1984). Alexithymia: Concept, measurement, and implications for treatment. *American Journal of Psychiatry, 141*, 725–732.

Taylor, G. J., Bagby, R. R., & Parker, J. D. A. (1997). *Disorders of affect regulation: Alexithymia in medical and psychiatric illness.* Cambridge, UK: Cambridge University Press.

Tromp, S., Koss, M. P., Figueredo, A. J., & Tharan, M. (1995). Are rape memories different? A comparison of rape, other unpleasant, and pleasant memories among employed women. *Journal of Traumatic Stress, 8*, 607–627.

van der Kolk, B. A., & Fisler, R. (1995). Dissociation and the fragmentary nature of traumatic memories: Overview and exploratory study. *Journal of Traumatic Stress, 8*, 505–525.

Wagenaar, W. A., & Groeneweg, J. (1990). The memory of concentration camp survivors. *Applied Cognitive Psychology, 4*, 77–87.

Williams, L. M. (1994). Recall of childhood trauma: A prospective study of women's memories of child sexual abuse. *Journal of Consulting and Clinical Psychology, 62*, 1167–1176.

Zoellner, L. A., Foa, E. B., Brigidi, B. D., & Przeworski, A. (2000). Are trauma victims susceptible to "false memories"? *Journal of Abnormal Psychology, 109*, 517–524.

MEMORY, 2008, 16 (1), 22–28

Psychology Press
Taylor & Francis Group

Linking thought suppression and recovered memories of childhood sexual abuse

Elke Geraerts
Maastricht University, the Netherlands, and Harvard University, Cambridge, MA, USA

Richard J. McNally
Harvard University, Cambridge, MA, USA

Marko Jelicic, Harald Merckelbach, and Linsey Raymaekers
Maastricht University, the Netherlands

There are two types of recovered memories: those that gradually return in recovered memory therapy and those that are spontaneously recovered outside the context of therapy. In the current study, we employed a thought suppression paradigm, with autobiographical experiences as target thoughts, to test whether individuals reporting spontaneously recovered memories of childhood sexual abuse (CSA) are more adept at suppressing positive and anxious autobiographical thoughts, relative to individuals reporting CSA memories recovered in therapy, relative to individuals with continuous abuse memories, and relative to controls reporting no history of abuse. Results showed that people reporting spontaneously recovered memories are superior in suppressing anxious autobiographical thoughts, both in the short term and long term (7 days). Our findings may partly explain why people with spontaneous CSA memories have the subjective impression that they have "repressed" their CSA memories for many years.

How people remember—or forget—extremely distressing experiences has been among the most contentious debates in the history of psychology and psychiatry (e.g., Loftus, 1997; McNally, 2003; Schacter, 1995). Especially prominent has been the controversy concerning the authenticity of repressed and recovered memories of childhood sexual abuse (CSA). As Clancy and McNally (2005/2006) have pointed out, many authors on both sides of this controversy presuppose that CSA counts as a *traumatic* stressor—an overwhelmingly terrifying event that almost by definition would be encoded extremely well. Yet empirical studies show that memories of traumatic experiences are usually extremely difficult to forget (Alexander, Quas, Goodman, Ghetti, & Edelstein, 2005; McNally, 2003). Accordingly, some researchers have argued that at least some instances of presumably repressed CSA involve false memories (e.g., Loftus, 2003). On the other hand, many clinicians have assumed that in cases of recovered CSA memories, special dissociative mechanisms have been operative, preventing these traumatic memories from emerging into conscious awareness (e.g., Spiegel, 1997, p. 6). However, a radically different scenario would

Address correspondence to: Elke Geraerts, Department of Psychology, Harvard University, 1232 William James Hall, 33 Kirkland Street, Cambridge, Massachusetts 02138, United States. E-mail: E.Geraerts@Psychology.Unimaas.NL

We would like to thank Dr. Amanda Barnier for serving as editor on this paper.
The writing of this paper was supported in part by a grant from the Netherlands Organization for Scientific Research (016.075.144) awarded to Elke Geraerts.

http://www.psypress.com/memory DOI:10.1080/09658210701390628

unfold if victims fail to understand their abuse, and fail to experience it as an overwhelmingly terrifying trauma. In that case, they may fail to think about the CSA for an extensive period, yet be reminded of it many years later (Clancy & McNally, 2005/2006; McNally, 2005). If so, this could be experienced subjectively by the individual as a recovered memory, but it would, of course, not count as a previously repressed one. That is, failing to think about something for a long time is not the same thing as being unable to remember it. Moreover, some individuals may forget having recalled their CSA, and this failure to remember previous thoughts and memories about the CSA may contribute to the impression of having repressed CSA (Schooler, Ambadar, & Bendiksen, 1997).

Recent research has yielded evidence for two types of recovered memories. Some individuals report having gradually recovered their memories of CSA during the course of recovered memory therapy, whereas others report having recovered CSA memories spontaneously after encountering reminders outside therapy (Geraerts, 2006). We found that the memories of CSA emerging during recovered memory therapy could not be corroborated, whereas those emerging outside therapy were corroborated just as often as memories of CSA that had never been forgotten ("continuous" memories; Geraerts et al., in press). This suggests that spontaneously recovered CSA memories are more likely to reflect genuine events, relative to CSA memories recovered during therapy. It seems likely that one source of the failure to corroborate memories recovered in therapy is that they are, in fact, *false* memories stemming from an interaction between expectations induced by therapists' suggestive techniques and intrinsic source-monitoring difficulties in their clients (Johnson, Hashtroudi, & Lindsay, 1993).

Evidence for source-monitoring difficulties underlying CSA memories recovered in therapy comes from laboratory studies in which adults with recovered and continuous CSA memories studied word lists. That is, adults reporting recovered CSA memories exhibited higher rates of false recognition for neutral and trauma-related words in laboratory tasks than did those reporting continuous memories of CSA (Clancy, Schacter, McNally, & Pitman, 2000; Geraerts, Smeets, Jelicic, van Heerden, & Merckelbach, 2005). Also, people who report having repressed or recovered their memories of CSA tend to exhibit poorer source-monitoring performance on a reality-monitoring task relative to those who report never having forgotten their abuse or those who report no abuse history (McNally, Clancy, Barrett, & Parker, 2005), and this relative deficit may be especially pronounced among those who report recovering memories of CSA during therapy, as suggested by post hoc analyses (Geraerts, 2006). Conversely, directed forgetting experiments indicate that those reporting recovered memories do not possess superior ability to forget trauma-related material relative to those reporting having always remembered the abuse, either when the item method (tapping encoding; McNally, Clancy, & Schacter, 2001) or list method (tapping retrieval; Geraerts, Smeets, Jelicic, Merckelbach, & van Heerden, 2006d; McNally, Clancy, Barrett, & Parker, 2004) is used.

Recovered memories imply by definition that those who have such memories have experienced a lack of continuous recall of their CSA memories. Some theorists have interpreted this lack of continuity as reflecting the operation of special mechanisms such as dissociation or repression that block access to these memories (e.g., Brown, Scheflin, & Whitfield, 1999). However, in their survey of nonclinical participants, Melchert and Parker (1997) found that a considerable proportion of those reporting recovered memories attributed their lack of continuous recall to intentional attempts to avoid CSA memories. Thus, a person may fail to think about adverse childhood experiences for many years, not because special mechanisms like dissociation or repression blocked access to the memory, but merely because the CSA was not understood as an overwhelming event, proper retrieval cues were absent, or the person engaged in prolonged attempts to avoid thoughts about the CSA (i.e., thought suppression).

In the experiment reported here, we adapted Wegner's (1994) thought suppression paradigm to test whether people with spontaneously recovered memories are better at suppressing emotional autobiographical memories than are those who report recovering their abuse memories during psychotherapy, those who report never having forgotten their abuse, and control participants who report never having been abused. Many studies have documented that attempts to suppress a target thought often paradoxically increase the frequency of the thought (Wenzlaff & Wegner, 2000). We asked participants to recall their subjectively most positive event and the most anxious event they experienced during the past several years (see also Geraerts, Merckelbach, Jelicic, & Smeets, 2006c). These two memories were the thoughts targeted for suppression. To investigate the long-term effects of thought suppression, we asked participants to record the frequency of the target thoughts for 7 days following the experiment.

Assuming that the CSA memories in the spontaneously recovered group are more likely to be genuine than those in the recovered-in-therapy group, we predicted that those reporting spontaneously recovered memories would be more effective in suppressing target thoughts than participants in all other groups. If the data conform to this pattern, then this may partly explain why individuals not in psychotherapy may believe that they have repressed a CSA memory when in fact they have not thought about it for an extensive period.

METHOD

Participants

As part of an ongoing research project on recovered memories (e.g., Geraerts, Jelicic, & Merckelbach, 2006b), we recruited participants with recovered and continuous CSA memories as well as people reporting no history of abuse, through advertisements in local newspapers. Participants were told that the research pertained to CSA and memory. CSA was defined as physical sexual contact ranging from fondling to penetrative acts until the age of 12. The study was approved by the standing ethical committee of the Faculty of Psychology, Maastricht University.

We conducted a semi-structured memory interview to classify participants into one of four groups. The *spontaneously recovered memory group* consisted of 30 (21 women) participants (mean age = 42.6 years, $SD = 9.1$) who reported that they had previously forgotten and then spontaneously recalled memories of CSA. The *recovered in therapy group* comprised 30 (24 women) participants (mean age = 41.0 years, $SD = 11.5$) who stated that they had recovered their memories of abuse during therapy. The *continuous memory group* comprised 30 (22 women) participants (mean age = 41.7 years, $SD = 11.3$) who said that they had never forgotten their abuse. The *control group* consisted of 30 (20 women) participants (mean age = 39.9, $SD = 10.4$) who reported no history of abuse in either childhood or adulthood.

Materials

During the thought-monitoring tasks, participants used a joystick button to indicate the occurrence of a target thought. For 7 days following the experiment, they also recorded occurrences of target thoughts in a tabular diary and noted its content (e.g., Holmes, Brewin, & Hennessy, 2004).

Intrusive target thoughts were defined as "spontaneously occurring" (not deliberate) memories about the positive and anxious autobiographical events. Participants were asked to carry the diary with them and record each relevant intrusion they had experienced. Additionally, they were asked to set aside a regular time each day to check whether they had completed their diary and to indicate explicitly when they had had no intrusions. The total number of intrusions was calculated from the diary entries.

Procedure

Following Barnier, Levin, and Maher (2004) and Geraerts et al. (2006c), we designed the study to have two stages corresponding to the two autobiographical events. Each stage consisted of an imagining period, a suppression period, and an expression period. Autobiographical events were counterbalanced across participants so that half of them first imagined a positive event, whereas the others first imagined an anxious event. Every participant performed the two stages of the study.

During the *imagining period*, participants were given 2 minutes to select and imagine the most positive (or the most anxious) event they had experienced during the past 2 years. To encourage participants to think about these events, we asked them to describe each event in writing. Additionally, participants had to rate the valence (0 = *very negative*, 10 = *very positive*) and the clarity/vividness (0 = *not at all clear/vivid*, 10 = *very clear/vivid*) of their memory for each target thought, as well as the distress (0 = *not at all distressing*, 10 = *extremely distressing*) and anxiety (0 = *not at all anxious*, 10 = *extremely anxious*) associated with it. During the subsequent 2-minute *suppression period*, participants monitored their thoughts related to the autobiographical events (i.e., target thoughts) by means of a joystick. All participants received the instruction to suppress the target event. Next, an *expression period* followed during which all participants were given 2 minutes to think about anything, including the autobiographical target event. Throughout the suppression and expression periods, participants indicated the occurrence of each target thought by pressing the joystick. Following this, they spent 5 minutes on a mathematical filler task, completing easy addition and subtraction problems. Subsequently, participants completed the second stage of the experiment by imagining, suppressing, and expressing the other autobiographical target thought. Finally, participants received instructions in the use of the 7-day diary and the distress and anxiety ratings associated with the intrusions.

RESULTS

Selected autobiographical events

The four groups did not differ in their valence ratings of the target events, $F(3, 116) < 1$. In general, participants reported more distress and anxiety during the retrieval of the anxious target events ($M = 5.07$, $SD = 1.86$; $M = 5.11$, $SD = 1.93$, respectively) relative to recollecting the positive target events ($M = 1.79$, $SD = 1.04$; $M = 1.17$, $SD = 1.12$, respectively). The groups did not differ in their clarity/vividness ratings of the target memories, $F(3, 116) < 1$, *ns*.

Suppression period

Table 1 shows participants' mean number of target thoughts during the suppression period for the anxious and positive events. The frequency of occurrence of the anxious target thought differed across the groups, $F(3, 116) = 4.56$, $p = .005$, whereas the frequency of the positive thought did not, $F(3, 116) = 0.25$, $p = .86$. Post hoc Least-Significant-Difference (LSD) tests revealed that the group with spontaneously recovered memories reported significantly fewer occurrences of the anxious target memory than did all other groups, $ts > 3.8$, $ps < .001$.

TABLE 1
Mean frequencies (*SD*) of target thoughts during suppression period

	Anxious event	*Positive event*
Spontaneously recovered	1.27 (0.98)	3.17 (5.05)
Recovered in therapy	3.97 (3.14)	3.57 (2.75)
Continuous	3.10 (4.09)	3.77 (4.89)
Controls	3.50 (3.04)	4.13 (4.61)

Mean frequencies (and standard deviations) of target thoughts for anxious and positive autobiographical target events during the suppression period reported by the four groups (each $n = 30$).

Post-suppression rebound effect

Table 2 shows post-suppression data for the four groups. A rebound effect is defined as an increase in the frequency of target thoughts from the suppression to the expression period. Hence, positive values indicate an increase in frequency of target thoughts across these periods. Once again, the groups differed in their frequency of occurrence of the anxious target thought, $F(3, 116) = 6.94$, $p < .001$, and LSD tests indicated that the group with spontaneous recovered memories exhibited a significantly smaller post-suppression rebound effect than did the other groups, $ts > 4.5$, $ps < .001$. The groups did not differ in terms of the frequency of occurrence for the positive target thought, $F(3, 116) = 0.05$, $p = .98$.

Intrusions during the 7-day period

Table 3 gives the mean frequencies of intrusions about the positive and anxious target events. The groups differed for the anxious target thought, $F(3, 116) = 40.57$, $p < .001$, but not for the positive one, $F(3, 116) = 0.27$, $p = .85$. LSD tests indicated that people with spontaneous recovered memories reported significantly fewer occurrences of the anxious target thought than did the other groups, $ts > 8.3$, $ps < .001$.

TABLE 2
Post-suppression rebound effect

	Anxious event	*Positive event*
Spontaneously recovered	0.47 (2.32)	2.97 (5.07)
Recovered in therapy	4.37 (3.20)	2.76 (5.70)
Continuous	3.57 (2.97)	2.93 (6.74)
Controls	4.10 (5.64)	2.47 (5.00)

Mean change (and standard deviations) in frequencies of target thoughts from suppression to expression periods (i.e., post-suppression rebound effect).

TABLE 3
Mean frequency (*SD*) of intrusions

	Anxious event	*Positive event*
Spontaneously recovered	1.50 (1.94)	2.40 (1.07)
Recovered in therapy	5.57 (1.38)	2.60 (1.10)
Continuous	5.40 (1.67)	2.63 (1.13)
Controls	5.53 (1.83)	2.57 (1.04)

Mean frequency (and standard deviations) of intrusions over 7 days for anxious and positive autobiographical target events.

DISCUSSION

The aim of the present study was to examine whether people reporting spontaneous recovered memories are better at suppressing anxious autobiographical thoughts relative to people with CSA memories recovered during therapy, people with continuous memories, and controls reporting no history of abuse. Results showed that people reporting recovered memories that are more likely to be genuine (i.e., spontaneous memories) are more successful at suppressing anxious autobiographical thoughts, both in the short and the long run (7 days). Unlike results of earlier research on repressive coping (Geraerts et al., 2006c), here this superior ability to suppress negative memories in the short term did not result in a higher frequency of intrusions in the longer term. That is, unlike repressors (Geraerts et al., 2006c), people reporting spontaneously recovered memories showed no rebound effect for anxious target events after 7 days. This is consistent with earlier studies from our group showing that people reporting recovered memories do not qualify as repressors (Geraerts et al., 2006d; McNally et al., 2004).

Note that our finding of superior thought suppression in those who have experienced spontaneously recovered memories fits nicely with the study of Melchert and Parker (1997). In their survey of non-clinical participants reporting recovered abuse memories, these authors found that a considerable percentage of them (23%) said that their lack of continuous memories resulted from intentional cognitive avoidance strategies.

As previous research (Clancy et al., 2000; Geraerts et al., 2005) has shown that individuals with recovered memories are especially prone to source-monitoring errors, one could speculate that different recovered memory experiences are mediated by different cognitive mechanisms. The current study suggests why people with spontaneous CSA memories may have the impression that they have "repressed" the childhood abuse for many years. That is, because of their superior ability to suppress unwanted thoughts, they may manage not to think about the abuse for several years. If many years later they encounter suitable retrieval cues, vivid intrusions about the abuse may then be experienced as a recovered memory. Of course, as we did not attempt to corroborate the abuse memories, one cannot make conclusions about the truthfulness of the memories. Moreover, even when an abuse memory is uncorroborated, one cannot assume that it is false. Still, actively suppressing traumatic events is not equivalent to amnesia for the event. Moreover, inconsistent with an amnesia account, we found that people recovering memories of childhood abuse episodes may have the impression that they have not thought about these memories for a long period (Geraerts et al., 2006a; Merckelbach et al., 2006). That is, they are prone to forget their prior rememberings of the event. Perhaps this so-called *forgot-it-all-along* effect (Schooler et al., 1997) and a superior ability to suppress negative events both foster the impression of having repressed the memory of CSA. When thoughts about the abuse enter memory, some individuals may successfully avoid thinking about the thought, and when they later encounter reminders of their CSA, their later recollection may lead them to believe that they must have repressed the memory.

One potential limitation of the current study warrants comment. We did not include a non-suppression control group. This leaves open the possibility that people with spontaneously recovered memories are more likely than other participants to be more compliant in following instructions. Yet there is no obvious reason why this group of participants would be more eager to follow instructions than participants in the other groups. Indeed, there are no significant differences among people reporting continuous memories of CSA, recovered memories of CSA, or no abuse history on the Marlowe-Crowne Social Desirability Scale (McNally et al., 2004).

Researchers should explore different pathways through which a person may forget and then later remember CSA. Previous work suggests that forgotten CSA episodes are often upsetting without being terrifying, as in classic traumatic events (Clancy & McNally, 2005/2006).

Nevertheless, attempts to avoid thinking about these experiences ("thought suppression") would certainly be motivated by the desire not to dwell on aversive, upsetting memories. In other cases, absent reminders during the period when the memories did not come to mind will likely be operative. However, absent reminders are not inconsistent with motivated attempts to forget. Finally, individuals may forget their prior rememberings, producing the illusion that the memory has not surfaced in many years. In conclusion, the possibility that recovered memories may not have been lost in the first place needs further study.

Manuscript received 29 October 2006
Manuscript accepted 20 March 2007
First published online 6 June 2007

REFERENCES

Alexander, K. W., Quas, J. A., Goodman, G. S., Ghetti, S., & Edelstein, R. S. (2005). Traumatic impact predicts long-term memory for documented child sexual abuse. *Psychological Science*, *16*, 33–40.

Barnier, A. J., Levin, K., & Maher, A. (2004). Suppressing thoughts of past events: Are repressive copers good suppressors? *Cognition and Emotion*, *18*, 513–531.

Brown, D., Scheflin, A. W., & Whitfield, C. L. (1999). Recovered memories: The current weight of the evidence in science and in the courts. *Journal of Psychiatry and Law*, *27*, 5–156.

Clancy, S. A., & McNally, R. J. (2005/2006). Who needs repression? Normal memory processes can explain "forgetting" of childhood sexual abuse. *Scientific Review of Mental Health Practice*, *4*, 66–73.

Clancy, S. A., Schacter, D. L., McNally, R. J., & Pitman, R. K. (2000). False recognition in women reporting recovered memories of sexual abuse. *Psychological Science*, *11*, 26–1.

Geraerts, E. (2006). *Remembrance of things past: The cognitive psychology of remembering and forgetting trauma*. Doctoral dissertation, Maastricht University.

Geraerts, E., Arnold, M. M., Lindsay, D. S., Merckelbach, H., Jelicic, M., & Hauer, B. (2006a). Forgetting of prior remembering in people reporting recovered memories of childhood sexual abuse. *Psychological Science*, *17*, 1002–1008.

Geraerts, E., Jelicic, M., & Merckelbach, H. (2006b). Symptom overreporting and recovered memories of childhood sexual abuse. *Law and Human Behavior*, *30*, 621–630.

Geraerts, E., Merckelbach, H., Jelicic, M., & Smeets, E. (2006c). Long term consequences of suppression of intrusive anxious thoughts and repressive coping. *Behaviour Research and Therapy*, *44*, 1451–1460.

Geraerts, E., Schooler, J., Merckelbach, H., Jelicic, M., Hauer, B., & Ambadar, Z. (in press). The reality of recovered memories: Corroborating continuous and discontinuous memories of childhood sexual abuse. *Psychological Science*.

Geraerts, E., Smeets, E., Jelicic, M., Merckelbach, H., & van Heerden, J. (2006d). Retrieval inhibition of trauma-related words in women reporting repressed or recovered memories of childhood sexual abuse. *Behaviour Research and Therapy*, *44*, 1129–1136.

Geraerts, E., Smeets, E., Jelicic, M., van Heerden, J., & Merckelbach, H. (2005). Fantasy proneness, but not self-reported trauma is related to DRM performance of women reporting recovered memories of childhood sexual abuse. *Consciousness & Cognition*, *14*, 602–612.

Holmes, E. A., Brewin, C. R., & Hennessy, R. G. (2004). Trauma films, information processing, and intrusive memory development. *Journal of Experimental Psychology: General*, *133*, 3–22.

Johnson, M. K., Hashtroudi, S., & Lindsay, D. S. (1993). Source monitoring. *Psychological Bulletin*, *114*, 3–28.

Loftus, E. F. (1997). Dispatch from the (un)civil memory wars. In J. D. Read & D. S. Lindsay (Eds.), *Recollections of trauma: Scientific evidence and clinical practice* (pp. 171–198). New York: Plenum.

Loftus, E. F. (2003). Make-believe memories. *American Psychologist*, *58*, 867–873.

McNally, R. J. (2003). *Remembering trauma*. Cambridge, MA: Belknap Press/Harvard University Press.

McNally, R. J. (2005). Debunking myths about trauma and memory. *Canadian Journal of Psychiatry*, *50*, 817–822.

McNally, R. J., Clancy, S. A., Barrett, H. M., & Parker, H. A. (2004). Inhibiting retrieval of trauma cues in adults reporting histories of childhood sexual abuse. *Cognition and Emotion*, *18*, 479–493.

McNally, R. J., Clancy, S. A., Barrett, H. M., & Parker, H. A. (2005). Reality monitoring in adults reporting repressed, recovered, or continuous memories of childhood sexual abuse. *Journal of Abnormal Psychology*, *114*, 147–152.

McNally, R. J., Clancy, S. A., & Schacter, D. L. (2001). Directed forgetting of trauma cues in adults reporting repressed or recovered memories of childhood sexual abuse. *Journal of Abnormal Psychology*, *110*, 151–156.

Melchert, T. P., & Parker, R. L. (1997). Different forms of childhood abuse and memory. *Child Abuse & Neglect*, *21*, 125–135.

Merckelbach, H., Smeets, T., Geraerts, E., Jelicic, M., Bouwen, A., & Smeets, E. (2006). I haven't thought about this for years! Dating recent recalls of vivid memories. *Applied Cognitive Psychology*, *20*, 33–42.

Schacter, D. L. (1995). Memory wars. *Scientific American, 272*, 135–139.

Schooler, J. W., Ambadar, Z., & Bendiksen, M. A. (1997). A cognitive corroborative case study approach for investigating discovered memories of sexual abuse. In J. D. Read & D. S. Lindsay (Eds.), *Recollections of trauma: Scientific research and clinical practice* (pp. 379–388). New York: Plenum.

Spiegel, D. (1997). Foreword. In D. Spiegel (Ed.), *Repressed memories* (pp. 5–11). Washington, DC: American Psychiatric Press.

Wegner, D. M. (1994). Ironic processes of mental control. *Psychological Review, 101*, 34–52.

Wenzlaff, R. M., & Wegner, D. M. (2000). Thought suppression. *Annual Review of Psychology, 51*, 59–91.

MEMORY, 2008, 16 (1), 29–47

Psychology Press
Taylor & Francis Group

Review of the contemporary literature on how children report sexual abuse to others: Findings, methodological issues, and implications for forensic interviewers

Kamala London
University of Toledo, OH, USA

Maggie Bruck
Johns Hopkins University, Baltimore, MD, USA

Daniel B. Wright
University of Sussex, UK

Stephen J. Ceci
Cornell University

Methods used during forensic interviews with children are driven by beliefs about how children recall and report child sexual abuse (CSA) to others. Summit (1983) proposed a theory (*Child Sexual Abuse Accommodation Syndrome*) contending that, due to the specific traumatic characteristics of CSA, children will often delay disclosing abuse or altogether fail to disclose during childhood, deny abuse when asked, and often recant abuse allegations. His theory has had a tremendous impact on the field of CSA forensic evaluations, despite its dearth of empirical support. In this paper, we review and critique the contemporary literature from two main sources: retrospective accounts from adults reporting CSA experiences and studies of children undergoing forensic evaluation for CSA. We conclude that data support the notion that children often delay abuse disclosure, but that among valid abuse cases undergoing forensic evaluation, denial and recantation are not common. Methodological issues and implications for forensic interviewers are discussed.

Child sexual abuse (CSA) is a major societal problem that presents an array of difficult decisions for those involved in its investigation and substantiation. In cases that come before authorities, investigative interviewers face the weighty task of evaluating the veracity of children's allegations. Errors in judgement either allow perpetrators to be free to commit further abuse or, at the other extreme, lead to the break-up of families or imprisonment of innocent people. In the absence of reliable medical evidence or corroborative eyewitness testimony, the diagnosis of CSA is complicated because psychological and medical profiles do not reliably differentiate abused and non-abused children. Psychological findings are inconclusive because many behaviours that might result from abuse (e.g., anxiety, bedwetting, sexual play) are also present in many non-abused children (Kendall-Tacket, Williams, & Finkelhor, 1993; see Poole & Lindsay, 1998;

Address correspondence to: Kamala London, Department of Psychology/ MS948, University of Toledo, Toledo, OH 43606, USA. E-mail: kamala.london@utoledo.edu

http://www.psypress.com/memory DOI:10.1080/09658210701725732

J. Wood & Wright, 1995). Medical findings are often inconclusive or simply not present because many types of sexual abuse, such as fondling, do not leave physical evidence. Even when there is some medical evidence it is most often inconclusive of abuse in that many non-abused children show similar findings (e.g., Berenson et al., 2000; Heger, Ticson, Velasquez, & Bernier, 2002; McCann, Wells, Simon, & Voris, 1990). Thus, in most cases the child's statement is the sole evidence by which fact-finders can evaluate the validity or likelihood of the allegations.

This reliance on children's statements has raised concerns due to two related factors. First, there is a general belief that a majority of CSA victims do not disclose abuse even in formal interviews. Consequently, when suspicion is high, investigators often feel it necessary to use an array of techniques to elicit the allegations. This leads to the second concern that the use of such techniques is suggestive and associated with a risk of eliciting false disclosures and false memories (see Bruck, Ceci, & Principe, 2006). The critical issue thus focuses on the need to use such suggestive techniques given the risk of false reports. In order to address this issue, however, one must first examine the validity of the belief that CSA victims do not disclose abuse, as well as the characteristics of victim, perpetrator, and crime that are associated with nondisclosure. This paper focuses on these issues.

CHILD SEXUAL ABUSE ACCOMMODATION SYNDROME

The major influence in formulating the issues concerning nondisclosure in CSA victims was Roland Summit's Child Sexual Abuse Accommodation Syndrome (CSAAS; Summit, 1983). Summit stated that, due to the nature of child sexual abuse, certain psychological factors (shame, embarrassment, sense of responsibility, allegiance to the perpetrator) often result in the behavioural sequelae of delayed disclosure, denial of abuse, and recantation of abuse. Summit's 1983 paper has exerted a tremendous influence on forensic interview practices.

However, models such as CSAAS were theoretical in nature and were not based on systematic observations or scientific studies. Due to concerns about the misuse of CSAAS as a CSA diagnostic tool, Summit (1992) later emphasised that his 1983 theory "... is a clinical opinion, not a scientific instrument" (p. 156). However, his plea for caution seems to have been less influential than his original paper. A citation count from PSYCHINFO (1 November 2006) reveals that 1983 paper was cited 139 times in other articles in the PSYCHINFO database; whereas the 1992 cautionary paper was only cited 9 times.

Given the non-empirical basis of the assumptions of CSAAS, London and colleagues (London, Bruck, Ceci, & Shuman, 2005, 2007) reviewed the evidence for CSAAS. They concluded that despite the widespread beliefs among clinicians and researchers, there was relatively little scientific examination of the theory, and either the evidence, such as there was, was methodologically problematic or the findings were equivocal. In this paper we update that review by adding new studies and by focusing on some major methodological issues that have posed barriers to the field of research examining disclosure patterns of sexually abused children and that must be seriously considered to advance knowledge in this field.

We focus on the two major sources of data that provide information about disclosure patterns. One source comes from studies of adults who report histories of sexual abuse. In one set of studies adults with histories of CSA were asked whether and when they disclosed the abuse to others; these results have been used to estimate delays of disclosure of CSA. The results of these studies are reported in the first major section of this paper. The second source comes from studies of children undergoing assessment of abuse. These studies are typically case reviews of children undergoing forensic evaluation or psychological/medical treatment; these data have primarily been used to provide estimates of denial and of recantation of abuse. The results of these studies are presented in the second major section. Within each section we focus on two main methodological issues that affect interpretation of the results: the reliability of retrospective recall of events surrounding CSA, and sampling procedures. We also discuss studies that did not present childhood disclosure rates, but do shed light on other important factors related to disclosure patterns. We limit our review to studies published since 1990, due to the many changes that have taken place in educating children about abuse and to major reforms in best practice guidelines for forensic interviewers.

DELAY OF DISCLOSURE: ADULTS' RETROSPECTIVE REPORTS OF CSA

Retrospective studies of CSA disclosure provide information on delay of disclosure during childhood as reported by adults who indicate they experienced CSA. We identified 13 studies that provide relevant information about rates of disclosure and delay of disclosure in childhood and one additional study that only includes data of disclosure rates to authorities only (see Table 1). In all these studies adults with childhood histories of abuse were identified and were asked details of the abuse, including whether they had told an adult about the abuse and if so at what time period relative to the abuse.

Major findings

As can be seen from Table 1, the sampling techniques and definitions of abuse varied across studies. Most studies employed convenience samples (e.g., college students, adults at sexual abuse support groups, respondents to magazine solicitations). Some studies only included victims of intrafamilial abuse, and some only included female participants. Some studies defined "abuse" generally, such as any unwanted sexual experience before age 18, contact or no contact, including by peers. Others defined abuse narrowly, such as incidents involving forcible penetration occurring before age 14 by someone at least 5 years older. There are also differences in the time windows used to define time of disclosure (e.g., "within 1 year of the abuse" vs "by age 14" or "by age 18").

Despite these methodological variations, some consistent findings emerge from the retrospective literature. First, most adults reported they delayed disclosure or altogether failed to disclose the abuse to anyone during childhood. Table 1 shows that, excluding two outliers (Fergusson, Lynskey, & Horwood, 1996; Fleming, 1997), the estimate of the frequency of childhood disclosure ranged from 31% to 45%. Stated another way, 55–69% of adults indicated that they never told anyone about the sexual abuse during childhood. Considering the range of definitions of abuse, sampling methods, sampling characteristics, and age cutoffs for "childhood disclosure" across these studies, these rates are remarkably consistent. A second consistent finding (see column 9 of Table 1) was the low frequency of reports to the authorities; the range was from 5% to 13%. Finally, a sizable minority of participants reported that the first and only time they had ever reported CSA was during the survey (see last column of Table 1).

These data indicate that, indeed, many childhood victims of sexual abuse do not readily report the abuse, and a fair number of them never report the abuse. These data are consistent with the CSAAS position that many CSA victims do not immediately report abuse.

Although delayed disclosure of abuse seems common, it is difficult to estimate length of delay because of between-study differences in measurement of delay (e.g., from the onset versus offset of abuse; number of months vs number of years) and because most of the statistics are limited to means and standard deviations. From a closer examination of the few studies that do report more detailed information, it appears that distribution of delay of reporting is positively skewed; many children disclosed within a month of abuse and then many waited 1 year or more to disclose. Hence, the mean length of disclosure provides a longer estimated length of delay compared with the median length to disclosure (e.g., see Kellogg & Huston, 1995). For example, Smith et al. (2000) found 34% of women who were victims of childhood rape disclosed within 6 months of the abuse; 18% disclosed between 6 months and 60 months; and 48% waited 60 or more months to disclose. Similar trends with different time periods were obtained in Finkelhor, Hotaling, Lewis, and Smith's (1990) telephone survey. Of those with histories of CSA, 42% reported having disclosed abuse within 1 year of the incident, 20% told someone of the event later, and 38% never told anyone of the abuse prior to the telephone interview.

In sum, many abuse victims fail to report the abuse in childhood. Even when childhood disclosures occur, there often is a considerable time lag between the abuse and disclosure. Based on limited data we hypothesise that many children disclose shortly after the CSA, with many more waiting a considerable time to disclose. Because of the right skew of the data the mean length of delay to disclosure does not provide a fair measure of central tendency. As a result, researchers should report more information about the distribution of this variable, including the median.

TABLE 1
Frequency of disclosure of child abuse recalled in retrospective studies

Study	*Survey sample (n =)*	*Survey sample CSA (%)*	*Sample source*[a]	*Mean age (yrs) at abuse*	*Mean age (yrs) at survey*	*Definition of CSA*	*Childhood disclosure rates*	*CSA reported to authorities*	*First disclosure at survey*
1. Fleming (1997)	710 (f)	20%	Australia electoral register Over-sampled those with an alcohol problem	10	39	Contact & non-contact abuse <age 17 by someone ≥5 years older	21% in first year 38% in 1–10 years	5%	10%
2. Arata (1998)	860 (f)[b]	24%	College sample	8.5	23	Unwanted contact before 14 yrs	31% (at time of abuse)	10%	
3. Smith et al. (2000)	3220 (f)	9%	National probability sample	10.9	45	Rape	34% (within 6 months of abuse)	12%	28%
4. Roesler & Wind (1994)	286 (f)	100%	CSA hotline callers	6	41	Intra-familial before 16 yrs	36%		
5. Lamb & Edgar-Smith (1994)	48(f) 12 (m)[c]	100%	Newspaper ad	8.15	30	Not specified	36% (by age 13)		
6. Mullen et al. (1993)	298 (f)[d]	100%	Random sample of women in a New Zealand town	<16	Ages 18–65	Sexual abuse in some form before age 16	37% within 1 year of abuse	7.5%	
7. Roesler (1994)	168 (f) 20(m)	100%	Abuse centre	<16	41	Genital contact before 16 yrs	37%		
8. Tang (2002)	1151 (f) 887 (m)	6%	Hong Kong Chinese college students	11	21	Unwanted sexual experiences before age 18	38%		
9. Finkelhor et al. (1990)	1481(f) 1145 (m)	27% (f) 16% (m)	National probability sample	Median =9.7	30–39	Before 18 yrs	42% within 1 year of abuse		38%
10. Somer & Szwarcberg (2001)	41(f)	100%	Israeli abuse centre	7.11	32	CSA survivors	45% (by age 17)		
11. Ullman & Filipas (2005)	733 (m & f)	22.8%	College students	<14	20	Contact & non-contact abuse <age 14 by someone ≥5 years older	45% <age 14 66.5% <age 21	13%	
12. Ussher & Dewberry 1995)	775 (f)	100%	Magazine survey	8.5	38	Unwanted sexual attention	54%[d]	18%	46%
12. Fergusson et al. (1996)	1019 (m&f)	10%	New Zealand longitudinal study	<16	18	Unwanted experience before 16 yrs	87% (by age 18)		
13. Hanson et al. (1999)	4008(f)	8.5%	National probability sample	<18	37.5	Non-consensual penetration assaults before age 18		13%	

Studies are listed in ascending order by rates of disclosure in childhood.

[a]Unless noted, all studies were conducted in the United States.

[b]Female.

[c]Male.

[d]The age by which disclosures were made in this sample was unclear but reactions to disclosing participants implies during childhood (see Ussher & Dewberry, 1995, p. 183).

Characteristics of disclosers versus non-disclosers

Some of the retrospective studies examined whether certain characteristics associated with abuse predicted delay of disclosure. We focus our review on analyses that test some of the assumptions of the CSAAS theory concerning the potential causes of children's silence. These include the child–perpetrator relationship, the use of threats, and the severity of abuse.

Relationship to perpetrator. The CSAAS was initially formulated to explain children's silence concerning intrafamilial abuse (Summit, 1983) although later it was extended to include abuse from a variety of perpetrators. Children abused by a family member, according to CSAAS, often delay disclosure because of feelings of guilt, loyalty to the perpetrator, fear of not being believed, and worry of the consequences to the family of such a disclosure.

The existing studies are equivocal regarding this hypothesis. Consistent with the hypothesis, Ussher and Dewberry (1995) and Wyatt and Newcomb (1990) reported longer delays to disclosure among familial versus non-familial abuse. However, the more common finding is that there is no significant association between relationship to perpetrator and CSA disclosure/delay (Arata, 1998; Kellogg & Hoffman, 1995; Kellogg & Huston, 1995; Lamb & Edgar-Smith, 1994; Roesler, 1994). We urge caution in accepting these null findings because of the relatively small sample sizes.

Threats. One explanation for children's failure to disclose abuse is that they were threatened by the perpetrator of the consequences of telling (e.g., "Your family will be hurt"; "Nobody will believe you"). There are few relevant data to test this explanation and the existing data are contradictory. Ussher and Dewberry (1995) found decreased disclosure rates among intra-familial abuse cases that involved violence and threats. However, others (Hanson, Resnick, Saunders, Kilpatrick, & Best, 1999; Kellogg & Hoffman, 1995) found the opposite; higher disclosure rates were associated with incidents that involved threat of physical injury. One study found no relationship between the reported presence of threats and disclosure of CSA (Roesler, 1994).

The major shortcoming of these data concerns the researchers' failure to define threats to their readers and presumably to the participants. Thus, it is not clear if threats were construed as force used to engender silence (e.g., "If you tell, I will kill your dog") or to gain compliance during the commission of abuse (e.g., "I have a knife and will kill you if you fail to comply"). At this time, there is insufficient evidence from the retrospective studies to determine whether the use of threats to gain compliance or silence affects disclosure patterns. Of course, the null and contradictory findings could be masking individual differences where some children view threat as a reason to disclose to prevent a possibly violent assault and others view threat as a reason not to disclose to avoid such an assault. The present data do not allow us to differentiate this from simple null effects.

Severity of abuse. Research to examine severity of abuse/use of force and disclosure has also yielded inconsistent results. Two studies (Arata, 1998; Ussher & Dewberry, 1995) reported longer delays until disclosure among more severe cases. Most researchers have either found the opposite pattern—that is, higher disclosure rates are associated with incidents that are life threatening and involve physical injury (Hanson et al., 1999; Kellogg & Hoffman, 1995), or there is no significant relationship between severity and method of coercion with disclosure (Lamb & Edgar-Smith, 1994; Roesler, 1994; Smith et al., 2000). However, investigators employ a variety of definitions for severity of abuse (e.g., use of force to gain compliance, abuse involving penetration), which could contribute to these null findings.

We just provided summaries of individual differences involving only three variables. However, the general pattern of inconsistency also holds for a variety of other psychological and demographic factors (e.g., gender, race), thus providing no strong evidence to support CSAAS or any other theory regarding children's disclosures of CSA. Further, even when adults in these studies (see Kellogg & Huston, 1995; Lamb & Edgar-Smith, 1994; Roesler & Wind, 1994; Ussher & Dewberry, 1995; Wyatt & Newcomb, 1990) provided CSAAS-consistent explanations of delay or of non-disclosure of abuse (e.g., fear, shame, embarrassment, guilt, fear of not being believed), when independently tested, these factors tend not to significantly predict who discloses and who delays. As described below, some methodological shortcomings of retrospective studies may have rendered the data too unreliable to produce any significant associations.

Shortcomings of retrospective studies on disclosure patterns

The first issue concerns the reliability of the reports concerning disclosure and the timing of disclosure; in more general terms, this is an issue that is common to all retrospective studies (Wright & Gaskell, 1998). In most of the studies in Table 1, adults were asked to recall details surrounding their abuse that occurred in their childhood. Given the long period of time between the abuse and the study survey, it is certainly possible that these adults have forgotten that they may indeed have disclosed abuse (to a family member for example). One would predict, therefore, that memories of disclosure would occur more often in samples of young adults and adolescents than in a sample of older adults. The youngest sample of participants (18 years) was surveyed by Fergusson et al. (1996). This was the one study that had a very high rate of reported disclosure, perhaps because the participants had not yet forgotten the details surrounding and following the abuse itself (also see Kellogg & Hoffman, 1995; Kellogg & Huston, 1995).

There is also a rich cognitive literature to support the hypothesis that one could forget telling someone about abuse regardless of the time interval. In their investigation of flashbulb memories, Schooler and colleagues (Schooler, Ambadar, & Bendiksen, 1997a; Schooler, Bendiksen, & Ambadar, 1997b) coined the term "forgot-it-all-along-effect" to describe the finding that people sometimes inaccurately recall to whom, when, and whether they reported an important life event.

There is also another literature on the accuracy of "dating" past events. A general finding is that "dating" errors increase as a function of the retention interval. Usually, the tendency is to "forward telescope" the event; which means to place it closer to the survey interview and further from the victimisation than was the actual case (Janssen, Chessa, & Murre, 2006; Prohaska, Brown, & Belli, 1998). In terms of the retrospective studies in Table 1, the problem is compounded by the fact that the participants recalled events from their childhood, a period during which their sense of time and accurate dating is still developing (see Friedman, 1993, for a review). For example, Friedman and Lyon (2005) staged two events for 4- to 13-year-olds, and then 3 months later examined their abilities to estimate the timing of these events. Although the ability to reconstruct the relative timing of events developed considerably during middle childhood, even 13-year-olds inaccurately estimated the time of events that took place 3 months earlier. Returning to the retrospective studies, if the adult did not have accurate temporal representations of the event as a child, their accuracy in recreating periods of abuse and disclosure is highly compromised when questioned in the survey.

A second concern that arises in some of retrospective studies is that a number of the participants claimed that they had repressed memories of CSA and consequently did not disclose abuse. Specifically, Roesler and Wind (1994) found 29% of their participants indicated that they did not disclose in childhood because they had repressed these memories. Arata (1998) found that 42% of the women who did not disclose abuse reported that there was a time where they could not remember the abuse. When asked about the circumstances regarding when they became aware of their CSA, about 6% of Somer and Szwarcberg's (2001) participants reported they spontaneously became aware of their abuse during psychotherapy. The inclusion of such participants in the retrospective studies raises questions about the reliability of their reports of abuse (and thus of disclosures). As discussed in other papers in this special issue of *Memory*, during the 1980s and 1990s, the dramatic rise of reports of repressed and recovered memories of CSA led to a large research effort to understand the basis of such reports. It seems clear that, in most cases, these reports do not reflect past trauma but are the result of a variety of factors that cause memory distortions. Thus the inclusion of such participants in studies of disclosure of CSA would act to artificially decrease disclosure rate and render these statistics inaccurate. Unfortunately, in most studies listed in Table 1, participants were not asked if they had repressed and/or recovered their memory of the abuse, so accurate estimates of adults reporting repressed memories across studies are impossible to determine.

A third constraint in the interpretation of the adult retrospective literature is that, although the studies indicate that delayed disclosure or silence is common among sexually abused children, these studies are uninformative as to the frequency with which abused children deny or recant abuse reports. This is because participants in these retrospective surveys were not asked whether as children anyone had ever asked them about abuse, and, if so, what they had replied. Thus, it is not known whether the high rates of childhood silence reflected the fact that survey participants had never been asked about abuse, or whether it reflected denial to abuse-related questions. Of course the memorial limits that affect retrospective questions mean that asking these questions of adults might be uninformative. In order to examine the probability of this latter outcome, the literature on children's patterns of disclosure must be examined.

CHILDHOOD STUDIES OF CSA DISCLOSURE

In this section we review studies of disclosure patterns of children who were specifically assessed or treated for sexual abuse. Thus, in contrast to the adult retrospective studies, all the children in these studies came to the attention of and were interviewed by the authorities. Studies that provided data on children's denials and/or recantations during the interview/investigation process were identified. As with the retrospective studies, we excluded studies published prior to 1990 because of possible cohort effects that could be due to the changes in interviewing practices and prevention programmes (for children) that have occurred during the 1990s. Table 2 includes information on 24 identified studies. When relevant we also provide data from these and other studies on the correlates of disclosure patterns.

Most of the studies presented in this section involved "chart reviews" of children who were interviewed by CPS, mental health, or medical professionals specialising in the assessment and treatment of sexual abuse. Children presented at these clinics or centres for a variety of reasons that included a prior disclosure to an adult, a suspicion of abuse by an adult or an agency, or the need for a second opinion or more extensive interviewing. Thus, across and within studies, there is great variability in the methods by which children were interviewed, in the information collected, and in the procedures of diagnosing child sexual abuse. Furthermore in some studies, as will be noted, researchers categorised the children according to the likelihood of abuse (e.g., highly probable, unclear, not abused); in other studies only children who met some prespecified criteria for abuse were included, and in still other studies the certainty of abuse status was not specified. Of course, as with the adult retrospective reports, the diagnosis of sexual abuse, whether as substantiation or unfounded, almost always comes with some degree of uncertainty. Some children may falsely claim to have been abused after undergoing suggestive, coercive interviewing; alternatively, some children may falsely deny abuse for a variety of reasons including pressure from a parent to do so. Substantiation of abuse is a thorny issue, and we return to this issue to discuss its impact on the disclosure data in a subsequent section.

Summary of findings

As shown in Table 2, rates of disclosure in formal interviews ranged from 24% to 96%. Unlike the retrospective studies where childhood disclosure rates clustered around 31–45%, the childhood studies are dispersed in their disclosure rates.

Ten studies included data on recantation rates. As seen in Table 2, these rates ranged from 4% to 27%. Factors that must be considered when interpreting these data are discussed in the next section. However, it is clear from the available data that, although there is inter-study variation, the frequency of recantation is relatively low and only occurs in a minority of children who previously made claims of CSA.

In the remainder of this paper we focus on factors that might account for and reconcile the extreme variation on disclosure rates and, to a lesser degree, recantation rates. First we examine potential individual difference factors that are associated with disclosure. Then we focus on major methodological issues that involve sampling procedures which must be considered in interpreting the existing disclosure and recantation data.

TABLE 2
Disclosure and recantation rates from child clinic studies

Study	*N*	*Ages (mean/range)*	*Disclosed in interview*	*Abuse to disclosure delay*	*Recanted*	*Type of interview*
1. Gonzalez et al. (1993)	63	(2:11–12)	24%		27%	Therapy
2. Sorensen & Snow (1991)	116	mode =6–9 (3–17)	25%		22%	Therapy
3. Lawson & Chaffin (1992)	28	*M* =7 (4–premenarchal	43%			Social worker
4. Carnes et al. (2001)	147	*M* =6 (2–17)	45%			CSA team
5. Wood et al. (1996)	55	*M* =5.7 (6–11)	49%			CSA team
6. Sjöberg & Lindblad (2002)	10	*M* =6.11 (4–12)	50%	2.2 yrs		Police interviews in Sweden
7. Bybee & Mowbray (1993)	106	*M* =5.6 (2–11)	58%		11%	DPS and therapy records
8. Cantlon et al. (1996)	1535	Mode =4 (2–17)	61%			CSA team
9. Sternberg et al. (2001)	98	*M* =8.1 (4–12)	63%			NICHD protocol
10. Gries et al. (1996)	96	*M* =8.3 (3–17)	63.5%		15%	
11. Stroud et al. (2000)	1043	*M* =8.4 (2–18)	65%			CSA clinic
12. Hershkowitz et al. (2005)	10,988	Mode =7–10 (3–14)	71%			NICHD protocol
13. DiPietro et al. (1997)	179	*M* =7.5 (1.4–22)	76%* (47%)			CSA team
14. Gordon & Jaudes (1996)	141	*M* =6.40 (3–14)	77%*[a] (73%)		5%* [a b]	CSA team
15. Dubowitz et al. (1992)	132	*M* =6 (under 12)	83%* (59%)			CSA clinic
16. Pipe et al. (2007)	397	4–13	83%			NICHD protocol
17. Elliott & Briere (1994)	399	*M* =11.03 (8–15)	85%* (57%)		9%*	Clinician
18. DeVoe & Faller (1999)	76	*M* =6.8 (5–10)	87%* (62%)			Social worker
19. Ingram et al. (1992)	33	2–12	87%*			APSAC style interviews
20. Keary & Fitzpatrick (1994)	251	Mode =6–10	91%* (50%)			CSA team
21. Bradley & Wood (1996)	234	*M* =10 (1–18)	96%*		4%*	DPS
22. Faller & Henry (2000)	323	*M* =11.7 (3–21)			6.5%*	DPS/Police
23. Malloy et al. (2007) children, 257 cases	217	*M* =10.3 (2–17)			23%*	Any attempted conversation with child about abuse
24. Kellogg & Menard (2003)	164	*M* =12.7 (7–19)	Not reported	Mean = 2.34 years; median = 18 months	5%*	CSA clinic

[a]The criterion for substantiation for our analysis was a classification of indicated by the state.
[b]The 5% recantation rate is among the 108 cases indicated by the state. Among their 6 cases with a sexually transmitted disease, 3 later recanted. Among their entire sample of $n = 141$, 12% recanted. Among any child to disclose ($n = 120$), 14% recanted. These figures must be viewed with caution because the original interview was a short medical evaluation and included as "disclosures" reports made by the parent.
*Denotes statistics based on cases classified as substantiated, high-probability abuse cases; the next figure in parentheses, if available, is the statistic for all children in the sample, regardless of classification of abuse likelihood.

Individual differences/predictors of disclosure rates

In this section we briefly summarise those factors that have most consistently correlated with children's disclosures of abuse. It is possible that differences in disclosure rates across studies may reflect the relative presence or absence of these characteristics in the study sample.

Gender. Some data indicate that males are more reluctant to disclose than females (e.g., DeVoe & Faller, 1999; Ghetti, Goodman, Eisen, Qin, & Davis 2002; Gries, Goh, & Cavanaugh, 1996; Levesque, 1994; Sas & Cunningham, 1995;

Stroud, Martens, & Barker, 2000; but see Goodman-Brown, Edelstein, Goodman, Jones, & Gordon, 2003; Keary & Fitzpatrick, 1993) although the social and/or psychological reasons for this difference are not clear. These data suggest that differences in gender composition across studies could affect rates of disclosure.

Cultural/ethnic differences. Several studies have examined whether disclosure varies according to race and ethnicity. Some data indicate that there may be more reluctance to disclose among Latina girls (Shaw, Lewis, Loeb, Rosado, & Rodriguez, 2001), Puerto Rican girls (Fontes, 1993), and African American girls (Elliott & Briere, 1994). These data suggest that lower rates of disclosure would be expected in samples that include more non-Caucasians. Unfortunately, such data are rarely available in the studies listed in Table 2. Many theorists have posited that such differences might exist (e.g., Futa, Hsu, & Hansen, 2001; Rao, DiClemente, & Ponton, 1992; Tang, 2002; Toukmanian & Brouwers, 1998; Wong, 1987) and we await further data testing racial/ethnic differences.

When studies include children from areas other than North America there is the potential problem of cultural differences in the reporting of sexual abuse. Although there are no data to support this hypothesis, nonetheless one must be cautious in generalising data from one society to another where there may be differences in attitudes, types of abuse, and supportive facilities, all of which would impact disclosure rates. For example, Hershkowitz, Horowitz, and Lamb (2005) collected data on an Israeli sample of children. Although the results are within range of many others reported in Table 2, this does not necessarily mean that experiences of abuse and the factors that led children to disclose abuse are similar across cultures.

Developmental differences. Rates of delay of disclosure and of reporting increase as a function of age (e.g., Cantlon, Payne, & Erbaugh, 1996; DiPietro, Runyan, & Fredrickson, 1997; Gries et al., 1996; Keary & Fitzpatrick, 1994; Sjörberg & Lindblad, 2002; Lamb et al., 2003; B. Wood, Orsak, Murphy, & Cross, 1996; but see Bradley & J. Wood, 1996; DeVoe & Faller, 1999; Gries et al., 1996). For example, Hershkowitz et al. (2005) divided their sample into three age groups and found the following rates of disclosure: 48% (3–6-year-olds), 72% (7–11-year-olds), and 82% (11–14-year-olds). Using a similar interview protocol as Hershkowitz et al. (2005), Pipe et al. (2007) reported somewhat higher rates of disclosure as a function of age: 63% (4–6 year olds), 76% (6–8-year-olds), and 85% (9–13-year-olds). These data suggest that studies with relatively older samples of children will produce higher disclosure rates than studies with relatively younger samples.

There are two major interpretations of these age differences. The first is that younger children may not have the linguistic or cognitive abilities necessary to recognise the abuse as abuse, or to recognise the purpose of the forensic interview and convey their experiences during the interview. This is illustrated by Sjörberg and Lindblad (2002), who interviewed 10 children who had been abused by the same perpetrator and whose abuse was documented on videotapes. They report that only 50% of the children admitted to the abuse when interviewed. In a more detailed analysis of the interviews and of the characteristics of the children, Cederborg, Lamb, and Laurell (2007) concluded that four of the children did not report because the event was not memorable and because of their immaturity (three of the children were 3 years of age at the time of the abuse). For example, child 4 was abused once when he was 5.4 years old. He was interviewed 1.8 year later. In the recorded incident, the perpetrator briefly touched the boy's genitals while talking to him in a friendly manner. When interviewed, however, the boy provided little information and did not mention being filmed or touched. This appears as though the child's failure to disclose was not due to a number of psychological factors (e.g., distress, fear, alliance with the perpetrator) but due to the fact that he did not remember the non-salient touching event. A second possibility for age differences in disclosure rates is there is a higher rate of non-abused cases (unfounded cases) among younger children who are brought in for interviews where abuse is suspected. This could occur because younger children often make ambiguous statements that seem to have sexual relevance but are misinterpreted by adults.

Relationship to perpetrator. For the adult retrospective studies we found no consistent relationship between perpetrator relationship and disclosure. The data are a little clearer for the child studies. Specifically, a number of studies indicate that closer relationships are associated with longer delays and lower disclosure rates (e.g., DiPietro et al., 1997; Goodman-Brown et al., 2003; Hershkowitz et al., 2005; Pipe et al., 2007; Sas et al., 1993; Sjöberg & Lindblad, 2002). For example, among a sample of cases referred for prosecution, Goodman-Brown et al. found longer delays between abuse onset and timing of police report in familial versus non-familial cases. In two studies (DiPietro et al., 1997; Hershkowitz et al., 2005) that reported disclosure rates among all children presenting for abuse evaluation regardless of abuse substantiation, lower disclosure rates were found in cases where the suspected perpetrator was a biological parent or parent figure. Pipe et al. (2007) only examined cases where there was substantiation of abuse; although the absolute levels of disclosure differed from those reported in the above two studies, the patterns of results were similar. In Pipe and colleagues' study, among cases involving non-parent perpetrators, the disclosure rates were 47% (4–5-year-olds), 76% (6–8-year-olds), and 98% (9–13-year-olds). The comparable figures for cases involving parent figures as perpetrators were 38% (4–5-year-olds), 58% (6–8-year-olds), and 84% (9–13-year-olds). Thus studies that include a greater proportion of cases with parent perpetrators (e.g., Hershkowitz et al., 2005) are likely to have lower rates of disclosure.

Following this line of argument one would also predict that recantation rates would be highest for children who have already made disclosures about parental abuse. Data from Malloy, Lyon, and Quas' (2007) study address this prediction. They included children facing dependency court hearings (i.e., removal from the home) as a consequence of their disclosures of abuse. Typically, these cases are also associated with low levels of support from the non-offending parent, who is often emotionally incapable of protecting the welfare of the child and who sometimes rebuffs the child's disclosures, pressing for recantations; low levels of maternal support are associated with lowered disclosure rates (Elliott & Briere, 1994; Lawson & Chaffin, 1992). One would predict that this is just the context in which recantations would occur frequently; in order to absolve themselves of guilt of accusing a parent, of being physically separated from their parents, and of trying to placate the non-offending parent, children would easily recant prior accusations. Also, Malloy et al.'s (2007) sampling method (dependency court cases) and definition of recantation (involving any documented formal or informal conversation with the child over time) might have allowed them to identify cases of recantation that other studies would have missed (see Malloy et al., 2007, for a discussion of these factors). As it turned out, only 23% of the children did recant. Although this is one of the higher estimates of recantation, one might have predicted much higher rates given the dilemma of this special sample of children.

Summary. Studies that include a higher proportion of boys, certain ethnic minorities, younger children, and parentally abused children with low levels of family support should yield comparatively low disclosure rates. Because most studies do not break down disclosure or recantation rates as a function of these variables, it is not possible to estimate the degree to which a combination of any of these factors can account for the variation of rates that are shown in Table 2. Although these factors might account for some variation, we argue that it is not individual differences but rather methodological features, specifically the sampling methods used, that account for the largest differences. The remainder of this paper focuses on this issue.

Rates of disclosure differ according to sampling methods

In order to obtain reliable estimates of disclosure/recantation, one must first obtain a sample of children who were abused. In studies of children coming to clinics for evaluation of abuse, therefore, it is important to categorise children in terms of the probability of their abuse status; if this is not done, then the resulting statistic is a reflection of the disclosure patterns of abused and non-abused children. Given these conditions, failure to disclose would be appropriate among the non-abused children. As discussed below, a number of the studies listed in Table 2 failed to differentiate abused from non-abused children, thus yielding data that are uninterpretable with regard to the issue of disclosure/recantation rates among abused children per se.

The issue then arises of how to design a study to include substantiated or high-probability cases of sexual abuse. Although a number of suggestions have been provided (e.g., see London, Bruck, Ceci, & Shuman, 2005, 2007; Lyon, 2007), some of these raise a related issue, namely the representativeness of the results.

In order to address problems of substantiation of abuse, some researchers have classified children in their sample in terms of the likelihood of abuse. Children meeting one or more of the following criteria (depending on the study) are classified as abused: perpetrator convictions, plea bargains or confessions, medical evidence, other physical evidence, and children's statements. Although the use of such criteria is a good start, it should be noted that there are problems with each of these criteria. First, the accused may be persuaded to accept a plea bargain due to the stress, financial burden, and uncertain outcome of facing trial. There are some accused who have been falsely convicted despite the absence of direct evidence to prove child abuse, and on appeal their convictions have been overturned (Ceci & Bruck, 1995). Although this may not be common, it does happen. Next, medical evidence is not always an accurate indicator of abuse. In the statistically rare case where genital or anal abnormalities are found, similar abnormalities can sometimes be found among non-abused children (Berenson et al., 2000). Finally, using children's statements as indicators of abuse to some extent is tautological in studies of disclosure. Children who make spontaneous disclosures with much elaboration (for example) are categorised in the "high-certainty" group. Then the analysis of the disclosure patterns of the high-certainty group indicates that the children disclosed spontaneously and/or with much elaboration (or did not deny). Clearly, then, there can be no single "standard" for diagnosing abuse in these studies. Rather it is best, as many of the researchers have done, to make the assessment based on a combination of criteria.

Lyon and colleagues (Lyon, 2002, 2007; Malloy et al., 2007) argue that there are critical inherent biases in studies of disclosure that sample children from assessment/treatment clinics and use the examination data as the basis for abuse substantiation. As previously noted, the studies listed in Table 2 include children who were specifically brought to a clinic, mental health professional, or law enforcement agency either because they had previously made a claim of abuse or because there was a suspicion of abuse that required further investigation. Thus, most of the children in each study had been questioned by someone (e.g., teacher, parent) about abuse prior to the formal interviews or therapy sessions. Lyon (2002, 2007) argues that these samples elevate the rate of *suspicion bias*—it was the children's prior disclosures that prompted the investigation. Suspicion bias can act to increase disclosure rates since the disclosure itself is what launched the investigation. *Substantiation bias* occurs when the disclosure is the reason that abuse is considered substantiated. Both forms of bias, Lyon argues, are likely if the disclosure is the main evidence in the case, which in the real world is generally the case.

Lyon (2007) proposes a solution to avoid problems of suspicion and substantiation bias. He proposes to examine children with validated histories of sexual abuse who have not made disclosures until directly questioned by the authorities. His sample of choice is children with gonorrhoea but who have not made a disclosure. He identified 21 studies from 1965 to 1993 examining gonorrhoea in children—he claims that these data allow one to calculate upper bounds of abuse disclosure (see Lyon, 2007, Table 3.1). Aggregating across studies, he claims that only 43% of all children disclosed abuse. Although the strength of this sampling method is that it lowers suspicion bias and substantiation bias, the sampling strategy has a serious limitation in that such children are not representative of other sexually abused children presenting for evaluation. As we argue, these data at most tell us about disclosure profiles of silent sexually abused children with sexually transmitted diseases (STDs).[1]

First, the study of children who have not made a disclosure and where there is low suspicion of abuse automatically removes from study the majority of children who present for evaluation at clinics or agencies. Also, this procedure will necessarily lower the disclosure rates, as reported in Table 2; this is because one of the best predictors of disclosure in formal assessment is previous disclosure (DeVoe & Faller, 1999; DiPietro et al., 1997; Gries et al., 1996; Keary & Fitzpatrick, 1994). Specifically, among children who made prior disclosures, 74–93% maintained the allegation when interviewed. In contrast, only 7–40% of children who made no prior disclosure

[1] In this paper we do not delve into disagreements with Lyon's interpretation or selection of studies. Briefly these include (i) reliance on studies that were conducted in the 1960s and 1970s where there was lower awareness and sensitivity to the problems of child abuse; (ii) ignoring data suggesting a large number of SA children might have been infected due to sexual play with peers (this would not qualify as child abuse as outlined in this paper); (iii) reliance on studies that were not designed to examine disclosure patterns but rather transmission of STDs; consequently disclosure of CSA was often an aside with few details.

disclosed at a later interview; these lower rates of disclosure likely reflect a combination of unfounded cases as well as children who deny valid abuse cases. Importantly, these studies indicate that consistency of response is not only a characteristic of children being assessed for CSA but also probably a marker of the accuracy of their reports. Although children making prior disclosures are not representative of all abused children, they are representative of most children coming before forensic interviewers. By excluding children who have made prior allegations, the notion is that we are examining the large percentage of children who usually do not come to the attention of authorities. As discussed below, this presents serious problems if we seek to generalise findings in order to guide interview procedures used to interview children coming before investigators.

A second problem with Lyon's strategy is the generalisability of data produced from studies of disclosure patterns of children with gonorrhoea. Imagine we were somehow able to randomly sample 1000 children with valid sexual abuse histories, and then only examined the subsample of children with gonorrhoea. This limits our sample to those whose abuse involved genital contact and where the perpetrator had gonorrhoea. Although gonorrhoea rates vary by age, gender, race, region (Centers for Disease Control, CDC, 2004), 2–3% of children brought in for sexual abuse assessment have positive cultures of gonorrhoea (e.g., Ingram, Everett, Lyna, White, & Rockwell, 1992). Assuming that all of these cases involved genital contact with an adult (rather than another child), this reduces the size of our large sample to about 25 children. Next, suppose we wish to select only those children who did not make any disclosures prior to the forensic interview (to be on the liberal side we set this rate at 40% based on the findings of Table 2): we would then end up with a sample size of 10, or 1% of the initial representative sample of children who come to clinic for assessment of sexual abuse.

Another alternative would involve selecting children from STD clinics rather than from sexual abuse clinics. Following Lyon's proposal, we would then interview children who had not made any previous disclosures of abuse. Their responses would provide our estimate of disclosure rates among CSA children. This was the strategy taken by Lawson and Chaffin (1992, see Table 2) who selected 28 participants from a population of over 800 girls with an STD diagnosis; these 28 girls did not disclose before or during their initial medical evaluation. Given the fact that this sample is only 3.5% of Lawson and Chaffin's entire clinic sample, it suggests that most of the children had in fact disclosed previously. Thus they selected the group of hard-core deniers. The finding that these children continue to have a low disclosure rate when first confronted about the abuse (43%) only supports one of the most established social psychological findings—that past behaviour predicts future behaviour.

Next, those children with gonorrhoea (who did not disclose) are not just the proverbial tip of the iceberg of non-disclosers, but they are also likely to be different from sexually abused children in terms of demographic and abuse/perpetrator characteristics. For example, epidemiological data indicate that children with gonorrhoea are more likely than the others to be abused by a young African American from the Southern US where gonorrhoea rates are high, and to have had repeated penetrative abuse. It is also clear that Lyon's (2007) selected database includes a predominant number of children from inner city or very poor rural neighbourhoods; these are not typical of the backgrounds of sexually abused children but rather abuse cuts across socioeconomic strata (Finkelhor, Ormrod, Turner, & Hamby, 2005; NCCAN report, US Department of Health and Human Services, 2006). Thus, any inference from this sample needs to be made about a very specific subset of children with CSA. Lawson and Chaffin (1992) recognised this limitation in their own data. For this reason (as well as their small sample size) they cautioned readers against over-extending their 1992 findings, stating: "In part because of the epidemiology of gonorrhoea in geographic area studied, the study sample is not ethnically or otherwise representative even of sexually abused children at this single hospital, let alone all sexually abused children" (p. 540).

In summary, different researchers have argued for the use of different sampling methods for examining disclosure patterns among sexually abused children. All the sampling methods have limitations, and ultimately the choice of sampling methods is contingent on the population to which we seek to generalise. Our interest in issues of children's reporting and memory of trauma is spurred by children's reports and memories in forensic settings, where by definition, there is a prior suspicion of abuse. In fact it is this situation that has generated most of the research in this area. Admittedly and clearly, the results of these studies do not generalise to all CSA victims, specifically to those who never make an allegation or who for a variety of factors never come to the attention of authorities and thus researchers. However, these studies do address the important issues of denial and recantation; namely, how do CSA victims react when directly questioned about abuse by authorities?

In the final section of this paper we return to the studies listed in Table 2. Using the arguments just covered in this section about the consequences of different sampling procedures, we attempt to account for the variability in the rates of disclosure and recantation among these 22 studies. We group these studies into four categories that differ in terms of the reported rates and in terms of the methods used to select the children. As we will show, disclosure and recantation rates directly reflect the sampling methods used in the different studies, as well as the validated abuse status of the children in the sample.

Studies of cases with dubious abuse substantiation and questionable interview methods (studies 1, 2, and 7). The studies with the lowest disclosure rates and highest recantation rates included samples of children from court cases where the abuse status of these children is highly questionable. Children in these studies were involved in cases that involved satanic ritualistic abuse (e.g., studies 1 and 2 in Table 2) and unfounded allegations against day-care workers (studies 1 and 7 in Table 2). The children in these cases initially denied abuse (and hence the low rates of disclosure) and only disclosed after repeated and very suggestive interviewing. For example, children in study 1 from Table 2 (Gonzalez, Waterman, Kelly, McCord, & Oliveri, 1993) were victims of the McMartin investigations—although this case was tried three times there was never a guilty verdict, primarily because the jurors viewed videotaped interviews of the children and their investigators (see London et al., 2005, for details; Nathan & Snedekor, 1995, for details of these cases). Given this background, it is not surprising that rates of recantation were so high; children were reneging on their previous false suggested accounts of abuse.

Sampling among selected populations or subsamples of nondisclosers (studies 3, 4, & 5). Children in this group of studies were selected from larger samples of children undergoing CSA evaluation because they did not disclose abuse when first questioned during formal interviews. Carnes, Nelson-Gardell, Wilson, and Orgassa (2001) and Wood et al. (1996) reported disclosure rates among children who underwent extended evaluation because they initially did not disclose when first interviewed. In both studies, fewer than half of such children disclosed in extended interviews. These reported rates do not generalise to forensic samples, but only to children who need extended assessment because they do not readily disclose. One of the concerns raised by these studies is the reliability of reports of children who are repeatedly interviewed about abuse. If some of the children in these samples had not been abused, repeated interviews (especially those with a number of suggestive techniques) could result in false reports (see Bruck et al., 2006, for research and cases).

One study (Lawson & Chaffin, 1992) presented low disclosure rates (43%) in cases that presented with medical evidence (gonorrhoea) where the children had not made prior disclosures and where no prior suspicion of abuse was noted. We spent considerable time at the start of this section discussing the strengths and limitations of such a sampling method. The main strength is that the method minimises suspicion and substantiation biases. The main limitation is that exclusion of all children who readily made abuse disclosures limits the generalisability of these findings to all children with gonorrhoea or other STDs. For example, Ingram et al., (1992; see Table 2 # 19) conducted a similar study at around the same time period. They included all children who tested positive for gonorrhoea; 87% disclosed a history of sexual contact in a formal interview.

Studies that report disclosure/recantation rates without regard to abuse substantiation (studies 8–12, 16). Some studies reported disclosure rates for all children interviewed in a specific assessment centre or clinic (studies 8–12). Disclosure rates vary from 61% to 83%. The lone study to report a recantation rate in this group, 13%, comes from Gries et al. (1996). Because there is no attempt to differentiate abused from non-abused children in these studies, the rates must be viewed as underestimates of disclosure rates; that is, an unknown number of children who do not disclose do so because they were never abused. Similarly, the recantation rate is difficult to interpret: it could reflect a change from a false allegation to a true denial, or it could reflect the change from a false denial to a true disclosure. To obtain the most accurate estimates of disclosure and recantation, one needs to calculate the number of disclosures as a function of the number of all true abuse cases. In the next section we report disclosure rates in studies that report information on abuse substantiation.

Studies that report disclosure/recantation rates according to abuse substantiation (studies 6, 13–24). Three studies (6, 19, 21) examine disclosure/ recantation rates in substantiated cases only. Six studies (13, 14, 15, 17 18, 20) examine disclosure/ recantation rates in samples of children who come to clinic for assessment of CSA and report disclosure rates as a function of the certainty of abuse. Finally, three studies examine only recantation rates in a sample of children who have already made credible disclosures (22, 23, 24).

It should be noted that each study differed in terms of the criteria used for abuse substantiation. These included: "indicated by the state", medical evidence, presence of STD, and team assessment of abuse probability.

With the exception of one study (Sjöberg & Lindblad, 2002), the rates of disclosure for substantiated cases ranged from 76% to 96%. For example, DeVoe and Faller's (1999) participants were interviewed at a multidisciplinary clinic, which sometimes entailed several interview sessions. Children referred to their centre included highly complex cases or cases where another opinion was sought from CPS. Although only 62% of the total sample made disclosures, this figure increases to 87% disclosure rate in the first interview when one focuses on the 47 cases with corroborative evidence (e.g., medical findings, material evidence, offender confession, and offender conviction).

The one outlier among this group of studies in this section comes from Sjöberg and Lindblad (2002) who reported disclosure rates among 10 Swedish children for whom abuse was confirmed by videotaped evidence confiscated from the perpetrator. Among the 10 cases there was no prior suspicion and no disclosures. Only 5 out of 10 children disclosed during forensic interviews. However, as detailed in Cederborg et al. (2007), and already reviewed above, four of the non-disclosing children might not have realised they were sexually abused due to young age or the nature of the abuse. Thus the published rate of 50% does not indicate children's resistance to disclose, which is generally the interpretation given to denial in all previous studies.

Focusing on recantation rates, with the exception of Malloy et al. (which was discussed above), the rates are very low (4–13%). We conclude that unless there are major external pressures on the child (e.g., removal from the family) most children do not retract previous disclosures when they are true. Even under circumstances of pressure, the recantation rate was less than 25%.

Before leaving this section, we consider the accuracy of the substantiation classifications and the effect of unreliable rates on the main outcome variables. So far we have mostly dwelt on concerns of overestimation of disclosure rates by sampling substantiated cases. But there is also the opposite problem if children who are not abused are classified into the substantiated group, either because they demonstrate ambiguous behaviours that are considered diagnostic of abuse (e.g., suggestive doll play that is not diagnostic) or because they display "soft" medical findings that are also present in non-abused children (see Gordon & Jaudes, 1996). If such children were not abused and deny abuse, disclosure rates will be deflated.

There is one final issue, and this involves the inclusion of children in substantiated samples who may indeed have had sexual contacts, but these were with peers (under 16 years of age who are within 5 years of age of the victim) and not with adults; this is particularly likely to occur in sexually active samples of adolescents. For example, both Dubowitz, Black, and Harrington's (1992) and Gordon and Jaudes' (1996) samples included mostly inner-city girls, up to ages 12 and 14, respectively. Data from the Centers for Disease Control indicate that the average age of first sexual intercourse for this sample is age 13 (CDC, 2000). Failure to disclose in these situations may reflect the child protecting him- or herself from illicit activity, and does not reflect feelings such as guilt or fear that may arise when the child is the victim and the adult is the perpetrator. Ideally, these cases should be removed from the analyses.

CONCLUSION

There is disagreement about children's willingness to provide details about sexual abuse. There are strong positions: some argue that most children do not disclose abuse, and for the minority who do provide information many of these will eventually recant this information; others argue that although a significant proportion of children will not willingly disclose abuse, when asked directly they will report relevant details that are not recanted in subsequent interviews unless there are strong outside pressures to do so. At first glance, it seems that each argument stands on firm scientific foundations. However, as we have tried to show in this paper, there are major difficulties for both approaches, but particularly for the view that denial and recantation are common; major problems concern the representativeness of the samples to children who come before forensic interviewers, the actual abuse status of the participants, and the reliability of recall data.

This does not necessarily mean that the alternate view is correct (low rates of denial and recantation) because there are also problems associated with the supporting evidence that primarily concern substantiation bias. In this paper we have attempted to show the types of evidence that have been used to address such issues and, in so doing, to point out the difficulties with any one approach. Given these caveats, we summarise the major conclusions, lessons, or issues that can be gleaned from our analysis.

First it is clear that, although there are many inherent problems in using retrospective studies, retrospective national probability samples provide the best basis for estimating population values of what percentage of children disclose sexual abuse. There is probably considerable error in the estimates, given that some adults may falsely deny abuse (inflating disclosure rates), or some might have problems in recalling disclosure or time of disclosure (deflating childhood disclosure rates). Memory issues also affect childhood disclosure rates: rates would be inflated when people forget experiencing CSA; rates are deflated if people falsely remember experiencing abuse due to exposure to suggestive influences. Despite these methodological difficulties, the overall pattern is that many children simply do not willingly tell.

Having agreed that many children do not disclose willingly, the next issue is whether they will also deny abuse if directly asked. Because we cannot conduct population-based surveys to address this issue (for example, asking several thousand children if they were abused in the last year, and if so did they tell anyone, did anyone ask them, and did they deny), we must rely on samples of children questioned about abuse and whose answers have been systematically recorded. This requires recruiting from centres that question children about sexual abuse. Thus, by definition, because a significant proportion of sexually abused children are not officially interviewed, the clinic samples will not be representative of the whole population, but they will be representative of children who are involved in investigations of CSA. For these reasons, we focus on forensic samples because it is these children's behaviours that have posed the major issues to the legal and scientific community. This is not to say that the plight of the silent children is of no interest, but they present a different set of challenges.

We have argued that, in order to obtain reliable disclosure rates in forensic samples, there must be evidence that the children were actually abused. One important factor in making these decisions should be the quality of the interview itself. Until the late 1990s there were few scientifically acceptable protocols (so the overall quality of interviews among the studies in Table 2 is questionable). However, due to the accumulation of scientific findings on interviewer bias and the effect of suggestive interviewing techniques (e.g., use of anatomically detailed dolls, selective reinforcement, repeated questions, repeated interviews; see Bruck et al., 2006, for a review), a number of these protocols have been developed (e.g., see Lamb et al., 2003; Memorandum of Good Practice, 1992; Poole & Lamb, 1998; Sternberg, Lamb, Esplin, Orbach, & Hershkowitz, 2002). Because these protocols avoid techniques that are known to produce false disclosures, and use techniques that produce high rates of true disclosures even from young children (Lamb et al., 2003), the results of studies using such instruments should be given high prominence in issues dealing with disclosure. Three studies listed in Table 2 (Hershkowitz et al., 2005; Pipe et al., 2007; Sternberg, Lamb, Orbach, & Esplin, 2001) provided disclosure rates of children who were interviewed with the NICDH protocol, due to suspicions of CSA. Since these studies made no efforts to classify abused and non-abused children, we argue that these rates reflect the lower bounds of disclosure rates among general samples of children who come to the attention of authorities and are interviewed with empirically based forensic methods. The pooled rate of disclosures in the studies reporting disclosure rates on substantiated cases presented in Table 2 is 85%.

These rates will change depending on the composition of the sample. For example, they will be slightly lower if a great proportion of children in the sample include young children (7 years and less), boys, or involve intra-familial abuse, especially with unsupportive non-offending parents. Rates might also be lower when samples include high rates of particular ethnic groups.

Disclosure rates will also likely vary across communities and over time, according to changing criteria that parents or other concerned reporters use to guide their decisions on whether certain behaviours justify forensic interviews. These sorts of factors ultimately affect the overall rates of true versus false cases to come before forensic interviewers.

Although most of the discussion has focused on disclosure of abuse, there are a handful of studies that examined recantation rates. What can we conclude from these studies? One conclusion is that recantation may stem from false disclosures elicited by highly suggestive interview methods. As already discussed, the highest recantation rates in Table 2 were based on studies of children who made allegations of ritualistic abuse and whose testimony was elicited by highly suggestive methods. Relatively low rates occur in studies that do not have these properties. Of course, this does not mean that children who have been sexually abused never recant; the current data indicate a small minority of these children do recant abuse. Malloy et al. (2007) found a 23% recantation rate among a sample of mostly Latina girls who were facing or had undergone foster placement as a result the abuse and/or had unsupportive non-offending parent—even with this high-risk sample, the number is relatively low. It thus seems that among sexually abused children undergoing forensic interviews, a majority will provide details; and even with repeated interviews, most will continue to provide abuse consistent details (and will not recant).

First published online 20 November 2007

REFERENCES

Arata, C. M. (1998). To tell or not to tell: Current functioning of child sexual abuse survivors who disclosed their victimization. *Child Maltreatment, 3*, 63–71.

Berenson, A. B., Chacko, M. R., Wiemann, C. M., Mishaw, C. O., Friedrich, W. N., & Grady, J. J. (2000). A case-control study of anatomic changes resulting from sexual abuse. *American Journal of Obstetrics and Gynecology, 182*, 820–831.

Bradley, A. R., & Wood, J. M. (1996). How do children tell? The disclosure process in child sexual abuse. *Child Abuse & Neglect, 20*, 881–891.

Bruck, M. E., Ceci, S. J., & Principe, G. (2006). The child and the law. In K. A. Renninger, I. E. Sigel, W. Damon, & R. M. Lerner (Eds.), *Handbook of child psychology* (6th ed.). New York: Wiley.

Bybee, D., & Mowbray, C. T. (1993). An analysis of allegations of sexual abuse in a multi-victim day care center case. *Child Abuse & Neglect, 17*, 767–783.

Campis, L. B., Hebden-Curtis, J., & DeMaso, D. R. (1993). Developmental differences in detection and disclosure of sexual abuse. *Journal of the American Academy of Child and Adolescent Psychiatry, 32*, 920–924.

Cantlon, J., Payne, G., & Erbaugh, C. (1996). Outcome-based practice: Disclosure rates of child sexual abuse comparing allegation blind and allegation informed structured interviews. *Child Abuse & Neglect, 20*, 1113–1120.

Carnes, C. N., Nelson-Gardell, D., Wilson, C., & Orgassa, U. C. (2001). Extended forensic evaluation when sexual abuse is suspected: A multisite field study. *Child Maltreatment, 6*, 230–242.

Ceci, S. J., & Bruck, M. (1995). *Jeopardy in the courtroom: A scientific analysis of children's testimony.* Washington, DC: American Psychological Association.

Cederborg, A-C., Lamb, M. E., & Laurell, O. (2007). Delay of disclosure, minimization, and denial when the evidence is unambiguous: A multi-victim case. In M. E. Pipe, M. E. Lamb, Y. Orbach, & A-C. Cederborg (Eds.), *Child sexual abuse: Disclosure, delay, and denial* (pp. 159–173). Mahwah, NJ: Lawrence Erlbaum Associates Inc.

Centers for Disease Control and Prevention. (2000). *HIV/AIDS Surveillance Report, 12*(1).

Centers for Disease Control and Prevention (2004). *STD Surveillance Report 2004.* Retrieved 15 November 2006, from: http://www.cdc.gov/std/stats/gonorrhoea.htm

DeVoe, E. R., & Faller, K. C. (1999). The characteristics of disclosure among children who may have been sexually abused. *Child Maltreatment, 4*, 217–227.

DiPietro, E. K., Runyan, D. K., & Fredrickson, D. D (1997). Predictors of disclosure during medical evaluation for suspected sexual abuse. *Journal of Child Sexual Abuse, 6*, 133–142.

Dubowitz, H., Black, M., & Harrington, D. (1992). The diagnosis of child sexual abuse. *American Journal of Diseases of Children, 146*, 668–693.

Elliott, D. M., & Briere, J. (1994). Forensic sexual abuse evaluations of older children: Disclosures and symptomatology. *Behavioural Sciences and the Law, 12*, 261–277.

Faller, K. C., & Henry, J. (2000). Child sexual abuse: A case study in community collaboration. *Child Abuse & Neglect, 24*, 1215–1225.

Fergusson, D. M., Lynskey, M. T., & Horwood, L. J. (1996). Childhood sexual abuse and psychiatric disorder in young adulthood: I. Prevalence of sexual abuse and factors associated with sexual abuse. *Journal of the American Academy of Child & Adolescent Psychiatry, 35*, 1355–1364.

Finkelhor, D., Hotaling, G., Lewis, I. A., & Smith, C. (1990). Sexual abuse in a national survey of adult men and women: Prevalence, characteristics, and risk factors. *Child Abuse & Neglect, 14*, 19–28.

Finkelhor, D., Ormrod, R., Turner, H., & Hamby, S. L. (2005). The victimization of children and youth: A comprehensive, national survey. *Child Maltreatment, 10*, 5–15.

Fleming, J. M. (1997). Prevalence of childhood sexual abuse in a community sample of Australian women. *Medical Journal of Australia, 166*, 65–68.

Fontes, L. A. (1993). Disclosures of sexual abuse by Puerto Rican children: Oppression and cultural barriers. *Journal of Child Sexual Abuse, 2*, 21–35.

Friedman, W. J. (1993). Memory for the time of past events. *Psychological Bulletin, 113*, 44–66.

Friedman, W. J., & Lyon, T. D. (2005). Development of temporal-reconstructive abilities. *Child Development, 76*, 1202–1216.

Futa, K. T., Hsu, E., & Hansen, D. J. (2001). Child sexual abuse in Asian American families: An examination of cultural factors that influence prevalence, identification, and treatment. *Clinical Psychology: Science and Practice, 8*, 189–209.

Ghetti, S., Goodman, G. S., Eisen, M. L., Qin, J., & Davis, S. L. (2002). Consistency in children's reports of sexual and physical abuse. *Child Abuse & Neglect, 26*, 977–995.

Gonzalez, L. S., Waterman, J., Kelly, R., McCord, J., & Oliveri, K. (1993). Children's patterns of disclosures and recantations of sexual and ritualistic abuse allegations in psychotherapy. *Child Abuse & Neglect, 17*, 281–289.

Goodman-Brown, T. B., Edelstein, R. S., Goodman, G. S., Jones, D. P. H., & Gordon, D. S. (2003). Why children tell: A model of children's disclosure of sexual abuse. *Child Abuse & Neglect, 27*, 525–540.

Gordon, S., & Jaudes, P. K. (1996). Sexual abuse evaluation in the emergency department: Is the history reliable? *Child Abuse & Neglect, 20*, 315–322.

Gries, L. T., Goh, D. S., & Cavanaugh, J. (1996). Factors associated with disclosure during child sexual abuse assessment. *Journal of Child Sexual Abuse, 5*, 1–20.

Hanson, R. F., Resnick, H. S., Saunders, B. E., Kilpatrick, D. G., & Best, C. (1999). Factors related to the reporting of childhood rape. *Child Abuse & Neglect, 23*, 559–569.

Heger, A., Ticson, L., Velasquez, O., & Bernier, R. (2002). Children referred for possible sexual abuse: Medical findings in 2384 children. *Child Abuse & Neglect, 26*, 645–659.

Hershkowitz, I., Horowitz, D., & Lamb, M. E. (2005). Trends in children's disclosure of abuse in Israel: A national study. *Child Abuse & Neglect, 29*, 1203–1214.

Ingram, D. L., Everett, V. D., Lyna, P. R., White, S. T., & Rockwell, L. A. (1992). Epidemiology of adult sexually transmitted disease agents in children being evaluated for sexual abuse. *Pediatric Infectious Disease Journal, 11*, 945–950.

Janssen, S. M. J., Chessa, A. G., & Murre, J. M. J. (2006). Memory for time: How people date events. *Memory & Cognition, 34*, 138–147.

Keary, K., & Fitzpatrick, C. (1994). Children's disclosure of sexual abuse during formal investigation. *Child Abuse & Neglect, 18*, 543–548.

Kellogg, N. D., & Hoffman, T. J. (1995). Unwanted and illegal sexual experiences in childhood and adolescence. *Child Abuse & Neglect, 19*, 1457–1468.

Kellogg, N. D., & Huston, R. L. (1995). Unwanted sexual experiences in adolescents: Patterns of disclosure. *Clinical Pediatrics, 34*, 306–312.

Kellogg, N. D., & Menard, S. W. (2003). Violence among family members of children and adolescents evaluated for sexual abuse. *Child Abuse & Neglect, 27*, 1367–1376.

Kendall-Tacket, K. A., Williams, L. M., & Finkelhor, D. (1993). Impact of sexual abuse on children: A review and synthesis of recent empirical studies. *Psychological Bulletin, 113*, 164–180.

Lamb, S., & Edgar-Smith, S. (1994). Aspects of disclosure: Mediators of outcome of childhood sexual abuse. *Journal of Interpersonal Violence, 9*, 307–326.

Lamb, M. E., Sternberg, K. J., Orbach, Y., Esplin, P. W., Stewart, H., & Mitchell, S. (2003). Age differences in young children's responses to open-ended invitations in the course of forensic interviews. *Journal of Consulting & Clinical Psychology, 71*, 926–934.

Lawson, L., & Chaffin, M. (1992). False negatives in sexual abuse disclosure interviews: Incidence and influence of caretaker's belief in abuse in cases of accidental abuse discovery by diagnosis of STD. *Journal of Interpersonal Violence, 7*, 532–542.

Levesque, J. R. (1994). Sex differences in the experience of child sexual victimization. *Journal of Family Violence, 9*, 357–369.

London, K., Bruck, M., Ceci, S. J., & Shuman, D. (2005). Children's disclosure of sexual abuse: What does the research tell us about the ways that children tell? *Psychology, Public Policy, the Law, 11*, 194–226.

London, K., Bruck, M., Ceci, S. J., & Shuman, D. (2007). Disclosure of child sexual abuse: A review of the contemporary empirical literature. In M. E. Pipe, M. E. Lamb, Y. Orbach, & A. C. Cederborg (Eds.), *Child sexual abuse: Disclosure, delay and denial*. Mahwah, NJ: Lawrence Erlbaum Associates Inc.

Lyon, T. D. (2002). Scientific support for expert testimony on Child Sexual Abuse Accommodation. In J. R. Conte (Ed.), *Critical issues in child sexual abuse* (pp. 107–138). Newbury Park, CA: Sage.

Lyon, T. D. (2007). False denials: Overcoming methodological biases in abuse disclosure research. In M. E. Pipe, M. E. Lamb, Y. Orbach, & A. C. Cederborg (Eds.), *Child sexual abuse: Disclosure, delay and denial*. Mahwah, NJ: Lawrence Erlbaum Associates Inc.

Malloy, L. C., Lyon, T. D., & Quas, J. A. (2007). Recantation of child sexual abuse allegations. *Journal of the American Academy of Child and Adolescent Psychiatry, 46*, 162–170.

McCann, J., Wells, R., Simon, M., & Voris, J. (1990). Genital findings in prepubertal girls selected for nonabuse: A descriptive study. *Pediatrics, 86*, 428–439.

Memorandum of Good Practice. (1992). London: Her Majesty's Stationery Office.

Mullen, P. E., Martin, J. L., Anderson, J. C., Romans, S. E., & Herbison, G. P. (1993). Child sexual abuse and mental health in adult life. *British Journal of Psychiatry, 163*, 721–732.

Nathan, D. & Snedeker, M. (1995). Satan's silence: *Ritualistic abuse and the making of a modern American witch hunt*. New York: Basic Books.

Poole, D. A., & Lamb, M. E. (1998). *Investigative interviews of children: A guide for helping professionals.* Washington DC: American Psychological Association.

Pipe, M. E., Lamb, M. E., Orbach, Y., Sternberg, K. J., Stewart, H., & Esplin, P. W. (2007). Factors associated with nondisclosure of suspected abuse during forensic interviews. In M. E. Pipe, M. E. Lamb, Y. Orbach, & A. C. Cederborg (Eds.), *Child sexual abuse: Disclosure, delay and denial* (p. 77–96). Mahwah, NJ: Lawrence Erlbaum Associates Inc.

Poole, D. A., & Lindsay, D. S. (1998). Assessing the accuracy of young children's reports: Lessons from the investigation of child sexual abuse. *Applied & Preventative Psychology, 7*, 1–26.

Prohaska, V., Brown, N. R., & Belli, R. F. (1998). Forward telescoping: The question matters. *Memory, 6*, 455–465.

Rao, K., DiClemente, R., & Ponton, L. E. (1992). Child sexual abuse of Asians compared with other populations. *Journal of the American Academy of Child and Adolescent Psychiatry, 31*, 880–886.

Roesler, T. A. (1994). Reactions to disclosure of childhood sexual abuse: The effect on adult symptoms. *The Journal of Nervous and Mental Disease, 182*, 618–624.

Roesler, T. A., & Wind, T. W. (1994). Telling the secret: Adult women describe their disclosures of incest. *Journal of Interpersonal Violence, 9*, 327–338.

Sas, L. D., & Cunningham, A. H. (1995). *Tipping the balance to tell the secret: The public discovery of child sexual abuse.* London, Ontario: London Family Court Clinic.

Schooler, J. W., Ambadar, Z., & Bendiksen, M. A. (1997a). A cognitive corroborative case. In J. D. Read & D.S. Lindsay (Eds.), *Recollections of trauma: Scientific research and clinical practice* (pp. 379–388). New York: Plenum.

Schooler, J. W., Bendiksen, M. A., & Ambadar, Z. (1997b). Taking the middle line: Can we accommodate both fabricated and recovered memories of sexual abuse? In M. A. Conway (Ed.), *Recovered memories and False Memories* (pp. 251–292). Oxford, UK: Oxford University Press.

Shaw, J. A., Lewis, J. E., Loeb, A., Rosado, J., & Rodriguez, R. A. (2001). A comparison of Hispanic and African-American sexually abused girls and their families. *Child Abuse & Neglect, 25*, 1363–1379.

Sjöberg, R. L., & Lindblad, F. (2002). Delayed disclosure and disrupted communication during forensic investigation of child sexual abuse: A study of 47 corroborated cases. *Acta Paediatrica, 91*, 1391–1396.

Smith, D., Letourneau, E. J., Saunders, B. E., Kilpatrick, D. G., Resnick, H. S., & Best, C. L. (2000). Delay in disclosure of childhood rape: Results from a national survey. *Child Abuse & Neglect, 24*, 273–287.

Somer, E., & Szwarcberg, S. (2001). Variables in delayed disclosure of childhood sexual abuse. *American Journal of Orthopsychiatry, 71*, 332–341.

Sorensen, T., & Snow, B. (1991). How children tell: The process of disclosure of child sexual abuse. *Child Welfare, 70*, 3–15.

Sternberg, K. J., Lamb, M. E., Esplin, P. W., Orbach, Y., & Hershkowitz, I. (2002). Using a structure interview protocol to improve the quality of investigative interviews. In M. Eisen (Ed.), *Memory and suggestibility in the forensic interview* (pp. 409–436). Mahwah, NJ: Lawrence Erlbaum Associates Inc.

Sternberg, K. J., Lamb, M. E., Orbach, Y., & Esplin, P. (2001). Use of a structured investigative protocol enhances young children's responses to free-recall prompts in the course of forensic interviews. *Journal of Applied Psychology, 86*, 997–1005.

Stroud, D., Martens, S. L., & Barker, J. (2000). Criminal investigation of child sexual abuse: A comparison of cases referred to the prosecutor to those not referred. *Child Abuse & Neglect, 24*, 689–700.

Summit, R. C. (1983). The child sexual abuse accommodation syndrome. *Child Abuse & Neglect, 7*, 177–193.

Summit, R. (1992). Abuse of the Child Sexual Abuse Accommodation Syndrome. *Journal of Child Sexual Abuse, 1*, 153–163.

Tang, C. S. (2002). Childhood experience of sexual abuse among Hong Kong Chinese college students. *Child Abuse & Neglect, 26*, 23–37.

Toukmanian, S. G., & Brouwers, M. C. (1998). Cultural aspects of self-disclosure and psychotherapy. In S. S. Kazarian & D. R. Evans (Eds.), *Cultural clinical psychology: Theory, research, and practice* (pp. 106–126). New York: Oxford University Press.

Ullman, S. E., & Filipas, H. H. (2005). Gender differences in social reactions to abuse disclosures, post-abuse coping, and PTSD of child sexual abuse survivors. *Child Abuse & Neglect, 29*, 767–782.

US Department of Health and Human Services, Administration on Children, Youth and Families. (2006). *Child maltreatment 2004.* Washington, DC: US Government Printing Office.

Ussher, J. M., & Dewberry, C. (1995). The nature and long-term effects of childhood sexual abuse: A survey of women survivors in Britain. *British Journal of Clinical Psychology, 34*, 177–192.

Wood, B., Orsak, C., Murphy, M., & Cross, H.J. (1996). Semistructured child sexual abuse interviews: Interview and child characteristics related to credibility of disclosure. *Child Abuse & Neglect*, *20*, 81–92.

Wood, J. M., & Wright, L. (1995). Evaluation of children's sexual behaviours and incorporation of base rates in judgements of sexual abuse. *Child Abuse & Neglect*, *19*, 1263–1273.

Wong, D. (1987). Preventing child sexual assault among Southeast Asian refugee families. *Child Today*, *16*, 18–22.

Wright, D. B., & Gaskell, G. D. (Eds.).(1998). *Surveying memory processes.* Hove, UK: Psychology Press.

Wyatt, G. E., & Newcomb, M. (1990). Internal and external mediators of women's sexual abuse in childhood. *Journal of Consulting & Clinical Psychology*, *58*, 758–767.

MEMORY, 2008, 16 (1), 48–57

Psychology Press
Taylor & Francis Group

The effect of emotional stress on involuntary and voluntary conscious memories

Nicoline Marie Hall
Aarhus University Hospital, Denmark

Dorthe Berntsen
University of Aarhus, Denmark

Clinical theories of post-traumatic stress disorder often claim that intrusive (involuntary) memories favour emotionally stressful material and that these memories come with more sensory imagery and emotional reliving compared to voluntary memories. However, these assumptions have not been verified experimentally. Here we obtained recordings of emotional reactions to aversive pictures at the time of encoding, as well as records of involuntary and voluntary memories of these pictures in a subsequent diary study. A comparison of individual ratings, obtained during encoding, of pictures recalled involuntarily and voluntarily showed that emotional stress at encoding increased overall accessibility, independent of whether recall was voluntary or involuntary. However at the time of recall, voluntary memories scored higher on narrative content and on measures of imagery. The findings are compatible with research on emotion and memory in general, but challenge clinical claims of differential involuntary versus voluntary access to emotionally stressful events.

Involuntary distressing memories of traumatic events, also called intrusive memories, are a central part of the symptom profile in post-traumatic stress disorder (PTSD; American Psychiatric Association, 1994) and theories of PTSD have focused on the role of intrusions in the development of the disorder (e.g., Brewin, Dalgleish, & Joseph, 1996; Ehlers & Clark, 2000). These theories have stressed the relevance of distinguishing between memories that are retrieved through a controlled voluntary strategy and those that are activated involuntarily (i.e., with no preceding conscious retrieval attempt). Several researchers have used "trauma analogue", moderately stressful visual stimuli to investigate involuntary memory processes in healthy participants and have used their results to advance clinical theories of PTSD (e.g., Ehlers, Michael, Chen, Payne, & Shan, 2006; Holmes, Brewin, & Hennessy, 2004). In line with this tradition, we used an analogue design to examine characteristics of involuntary and voluntary memories of stressful pictures.

Most clinical theories of PTSD hold that there is a discrepancy between voluntary and involuntary memories regarding the effects of emotional arousal during encoding, whereas findings from research on memory and emotion in general would not lead to such prediction. These two contrasting views are depicted in Figure 1. The clinical view is illustrated in the top panel of the figure. In this view, the intense emotional arousal

Address correspondence to: Nicoline Marie Hall, Forskningsklinikken for Funktionelle lidelser (Research Clinic for Functional Disorders), Aarhus Sygehus, Noerrebrogade 44, 8000 Aarhus C, Denmark. E-mail: nicolinehall@gmail.com

The work reported here was supported by a grant from the Danish Research Council for Culture, Cognition and Communication, and by a grant from the Danish National Research Foundation. Thanks to Anne Stærk Jacobsen for help with the scoring of the data.
This article was accepted for publication as a brief report.

http://www.psypress.com/memory DOI:10.1080/09658210701333271

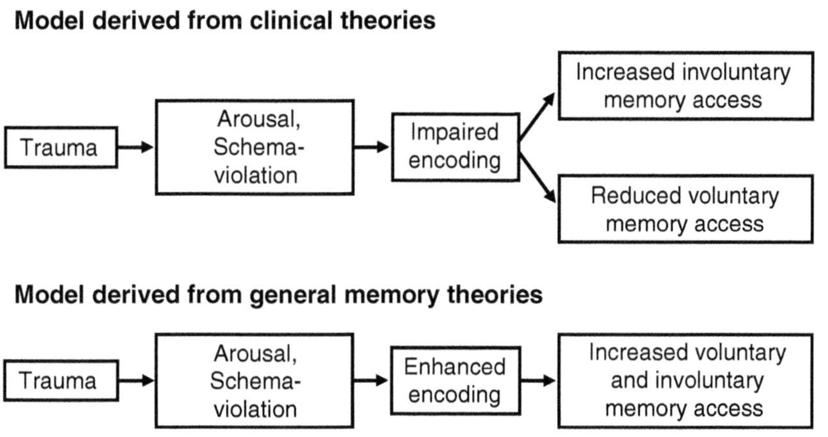

Figure 1. Predictions regarding stress response characteristics of involuntary and voluntary memories according to clinical theory and general memory theory.

and schema violation caused by the traumatic event leads to a reduced cognitive processing of the trauma. As a consequence, the memory of the trauma becomes poorly integrated with pre-existing knowledge and is hard to access through a controlled, voluntary search and retrieval strategy, either due to defence mechanisms such as avoidance (e.g., Foa & Riggs, 1995; Horowitz, 1975, 1986a) or due to the special characteristics of the cognitive organisation of the event in memory (Brewin et al., 1996; Ehlers & Clark, 2000; Foa & Rothbaum, 1998; van der Kolk & Fisler, 1995). While access through voluntary retrieval is impaired, involuntary access is enhanced. This view is summarised by Halligan, Clark, and Ehlers (2002) as a "pattern of poor intentional recall and easy triggering of involuntary memories" (p. 74). Accordingly, it may be predicted that negative emotional stress during encoding reduces accessibility for voluntary recall and increases access for involuntary recall.

Alternatively, according to a model derived from general memory theory (bottom panel of Figure 1), emotional arousal enhances encoding and consolidation in general and thereby increases subsequent accessibility of the memory (e.g., Bradley, Greenwald, Petry, & Lang, 1992; Cahill & Alkire, 2003; Cahill, Gorski, & Le, 2003 Christianson, 1992; Dolcos, LaBar, & Cabeza, 2004, 2005; See McGaugh, 2004). The effect of emotion on memory performance is demonstrated in animal learning studies (McGaugh, 2004, for a review) and in humans mainly through intentional retrieval paradigms (e.g., Dolcos et al., 2004, 2005). Based on general memory theory, we see no theoretical reason to expect a discrepancy between voluntary and involuntary recall regarding the effects of increased emotional arousal. Thus, increased emotionality at encoding should be associated with increased access for both types of recall.

The two approaches depicted in Figure 1 also hold different predictions regarding the phenomenological qualities of the voluntary and involuntary memories. According to the clinical theories, sensory details—predominantly visual impressions—will be particularly dominant in involuntary recollections. No similar prediction can be derived from general memory research. On the contrary, it has been shown that voluntary retrieval of autobiographical memories relies heavily on the visual modality and that visual imagery is strongly related to a sense of reliving during voluntary retrieval of memories (Greenberg & Rubin, 2003; Rubin, 2005, 2007). According to clinical theories, involuntary trauma memories involve more emotional reaction at recall than voluntary memories. Our previous work (Berntsen & Hall, 2004) shows that this applies to involuntary autobiographical memories in general. It is therefore not a trauma-specific characteristic but may reflect that a goal-directed retrieval attempt reduces access to the emotional content of the remembered event, (e.g., Conway & Pleydell-Pearce, 2000) or that voluntary recall involves more emotion regulation and thus less instantaneous emotional reaction to the memories (e.g., Gross, 2001).

In order to examine whether emotional stress experienced at encoding has differential effects on characteristics of involuntary and voluntary memories, measures of subjective reactions should be obtained both at encoding and recall, and voluntary and involuntary memories should be examined under comparable conditions. No previous studies satisfy these requirements. Several studies have lacked an involuntary memory condition (e.g., Arntz, de Groot, & Kindt, 2005; Berntsen, Willert, & Rubin, 2003; Geraerts et al., 2007; Porter & Birt, 2001; Rubin, Feldman, & Beckham, 2004) or an appropriately matched voluntary memory condition (Berntsen, 2001; Brewin & Saunders, 2001; Davies & Clark, 1998; Halligan et al., 2002; Holmes et al., 2004; Horowitz, 1975, 1986a). In addition, most studies have not obtained measures of emotional reactions in response to identifiable stimuli during encoding (e.g., Brewin & Saunders, 2001; Davies & Clark, 1998; Horowitz, 1975, 1986a).

The significance of individual differences is an important issue in PTSD research, and especially the propensity to dissociation has been associated with the proposed special properties of the traumatic memories of PTSD patients (e.g., Cooper, Yuille, & Kennedy, 2002; Ehlers & Clark, 2000). Individual differences regarding the frequency of intrusions have been studied (e.g., Davies & Clark, 1998). However, no studies have examined individual differences in relation to specific characteristics of intrusions or whether individual differences have different or similar effects on involuntary and voluntary memories.

To help remedy this lack, we here examined characteristics of involuntary and voluntary memories for negative emotional stimuli. We used distinctive aversive pictures as stimuli, which allowed us to measure subjective reactions both at encoding and recall. Phenomenological ratings of involuntary and voluntary memories were collected using a modification of the structured diary method used by Berntsen and Hall (2004). For each memory, our participants wrote a brief description of the recalled picture, which enabled us to later identify the source of the memories and thereby relate data obtained during encoding to data obtained during recall. Because we obtained measures of emotional reaction for each person in response to each picture at the time of encoding, and because we were able to identify which pictures were subsequently remembered involuntarily and voluntarily, we were able to examine whether the frequency of involuntary versus voluntary recall of pictures in the diary study was differentially related to level of emotional stress at encoding, as predicted by clinical theories. Because we obtained measures of subjective memory characteristics of the two classes of memory at the time of recall, we were able to directly examine the claim that involuntary memories involve more visual sensory imagery and more emotional reactivity than voluntary memories.

We measured individual differences with a series of questionnaires related to dissociation, PTSD symptomatology, anxiety, and ability to form mental imagery, in order to investigate the relationship between these measures and the phenomenological properties of involuntary and voluntary memories. As an independent measure of participants' propensity to experience involuntary memories, we used a thought suppression task (Wegner, 1989), which we expected to be positively related to the number of involuntary memories recorded in the diary study.

METHOD

Participants

A total of 129 Danish psychology majors (108 females; mean age = 26.0, range 21–48, $SD = 5.0$) participated in the study as a part of course requirements. The questionnaire, encoding, and avoidance sessions were carried out as a group session in an auditorium, whereas the diary task was carried out in each participant's natural environment during the following week. The participants were strongly encouraged, but not forced, to complete the diary. Not all participants handed in a diary (see later).

Questionnaires

The participants first completed a series of questionnaires: The 20-item Centrality of Event Scale (CES; Berntsen & Rubin, 2006), which measures how central a stressful event is to a person's identity and life story; the PTSD Checklist (PCL; Blanchard, Jones-Alexander, Buckley, & Forneris, 1996; Weathers, Litz, Herman, Huska, & Keane, 1993), a self-report rating scale for assessing PTSD; the Dissociative Experiences Scale (DES; Bernstein & Putnam, 1986), which measures the tendency towards dissociation, i.e., the lack of integration of thoughts, feelings, and experiences in consciousness and memory; Spielberger's State-Trait Anxiety Inventory (STAI-S and STAI-T; Spielberger, Gorsuch,

Lushene, Vagg, & Jacobs, 1983), measuring a person's present and general anxiety level; and the Vividness of Visual Imagery Questionnaire (VVIQ; Marks, 1989), which measures the ability to form vivid mental images (lower scores are related to higher imagery ability).

Encoding session

The participants viewed a series of 20 highly aversive pictures, 10 of which were selected from the International Affective Picture System (Lang, Bradley, & Cuthbert, 1995), 6 from the Empathy Picture System (Geday, Gjedde, Boldsen, & Kupers, 2003), and 4 from sources on the Internet. Several sources were used because of a need for clearly distinguishable and at the same time highly unpleasant stimuli. With the exception of two (picturing snakes and maggots), all pictures depicted traumatic scenes involving death and/or physical injury.

Each picture was presented twice for 6 seconds on a big screen. After the first presentation of a picture, participants rated their emotional reactions to the picture on dimensions of intensity, valence, dislike, bodily reaction, and mood impact and they estimated the self-relevance of the picture, all on Likert-type 7-point scales. After rating a picture, the participants viewed the same picture again and wrote a short sentence describing the picture.

After the encoding session, a thought suppression task (Wegner, 1989) was presented in which participants were told *not* to think of the pictures during the following 5 minutes but to mark down if and when a picture nonetheless did pop up in their mind.

Diary task

In the auditorium, participants received verbal as well as written instructions for the diary part of the study. On the same day and on each of the following 4 days they were to record one voluntary (intentionally recalled) memory for one of the presented pictures. In a booklet with a separate page for each memory, participants were to write a few cue words describing the recalled picture and rate their memory on 10 dimensions using 7-point scales. The variables were specificity (i.e., memory for a specific picture vs a mixture of impressions from several pictures), vividness, colour intensity, and degree of detail of the memory representation; valence and intensity of the subject's emotional experience related to the memory; and experience of travelling back in time, bodily reaction, mood impact, and self-relevance. In addition to the voluntary memory task, the participants were to pay attention to any involuntary ("spontaneously occurring") memories of the pictures. Involuntary memories were defined as memories that were brought to consciousness with no preceding conscious attempts at retrieval, either arising "out of the blue" or as an association to something in the environment or in the person's thoughts. Participants filled in a questionnaire, identical to the one used for voluntary memories, for the first picture (if any) that popped up in their minds each day. In addition, they were asked to indicate (with Yes/No responses) whether the memory had identifiable cues in their surroundings or thoughts. On the last page, participants were asked a few questions probing their general experience of conducting the diary. The participants were instructed to carry the diary booklet with them at all times and to record their memories as soon as they occurred.

Scoring

The key word phrases in the diary booklets were scored against the 20 pictures by two judges. The scoring included an "unscorable" option for cases with insufficient information. The judges agreed in 92% of the cases, and cases of disagreement were solved by discussion. An examination of the key word phrases showed that the participants often characterised the memories with information that went beyond the information given in the pictures—such as characterising a young man sitting besides three dead bodies as a brother in grief, although this relationship information was not present in the picture. Two judges categorised the pictures according to whether or not, at first sight, they afforded a narrative description. They agreed in 16 of the 20 cases (80%) and cases of disagreement were easily solved by discussion. Of the 20 pictures, 9 were deemed narrative.

Analyses

Most of the analyses to be reported involved multiple observations from each participant. Consequently, each discrete observation could not be treated as statistically independent. This problem was countered by ANOVAs and *t*-tests based on means calculated within each participant. In order to calculate means within each participant, only participants with at least two pairs of involuntary/voluntary memories were included in these analyses. Many analyses are therefore based on the 64 participants who satisfied this criterion or on 52 participants who satisfied this criterion and whose records all referred to identifiable pictures. None of the two samples differed from the rest regarding variables of relevance for the particular analyses.

RESULTS

A diary booklet was handed in by 109 participants. The mean numbers of involuntary and voluntary memories recorded were 2.18 ($SD = 1.57$) and 4.49 ($SD = 1.12$), respectively. Of the 109 participants who handed in a diary booklet, 17 recorded no involuntary memories. These 17 participants also reported fewer intrusions in the avoidance task and found the diary task slightly harder to accomplish than participants who recorded one or more involuntary memories in the diary ($ps < .05$). No other differences were observed. For all 109 participants, the number of involuntary memories recorded in the diary correlated weakly with number of intrusions in the avoidance task, $r(99) = .22$, $p < .05$, and with the DES, $r(99) = .26$, $p < .05$.

Figure 2 shows that the number of involuntary memory records dropped systematically over the 5 days. No similar drop was observed for the voluntary memories, except for a slight drop-out from Day 1 to Day 2. This can be seen to suggest that the reduction of involuntary memory records was due to decreasing accessibility of the pictures for involuntary recall over the 5-day period rather than decreasing compliance with the task.

Generally, there was a lot of variation in which pictures were recorded as memories in diary study. In only 6% of the cases was the same picture recorded as a voluntary and as an involuntary memory on the same day by the same participant.

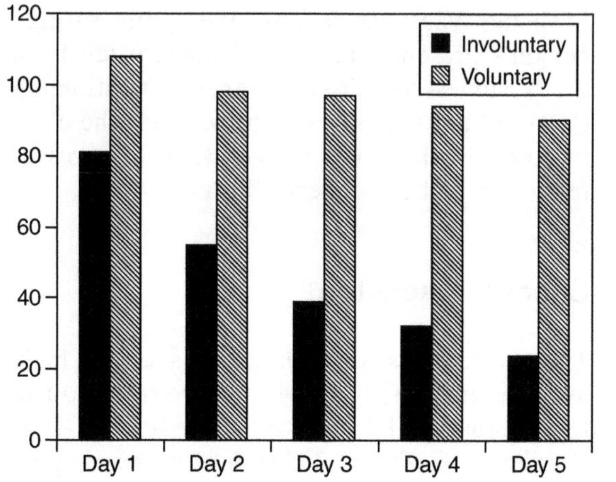

Figure 2. Number of involuntary and voluntary memories recorded on five consecutive days.

Of 227 recorded involuntary memories, 160 (70%) were reported to have identifiable cues in the surroundings or in the person's thoughts. This agrees with findings on involuntary autobiographical memories (see Berntsen, 2007, for a review) and with observations on intrusive memories for traumatic events (Ehlers & Clark, 2000).

Memory frequency as a function of encoding quality and narrative content

The 20 pictures varied widely with respect to ratings obtained at encoding (*F*s ranging from 79.14 for intensity to 12.89 for self-relevance, all $ps < .0001$). This allowed us to examine whether the frequency with which the pictures were remembered in the diary study varied as a function of their emotionality assessed at encoding. Table 1 shows the correlations between the frequency with which each of the 20 pictures was recorded (in voluntary and involuntary recall) and their mean ratings on the six encoding variables. To ensure comparability between the two types of memories, all voluntary memories with no involuntary memory from the same day were left out. Table 1 shows a remarkably similar pattern for the two types of recall. Pictures that were rated as more emotional and more self-relevant were recorded more frequently in both types of recall. Because the analysis was based on the 20 pictures as cases, and thus had little statistical power, this systematic pattern was only statistically significant for two measures.

TABLE 1
Memory records and mean ratings at encoding

	Memory records	
Encoding	*Involuntary*	*Voluntary*
Intensity	.44	.43
Valence	−.41	−.36
Mood Impact	−.31	−.27
Dislike	.52*	.45*
Bodily reaction	.48*	.44*
Self relevance	.37	.40

Correlations between number of memory records (voluntary and involuntary) for the pictures and their mean ratings at encoding ($N = 20$). *$p < .05$

In a more detailed analysis of the same issue, we calculated within each participant the means of the six encoding variables for pictures that were recalled versus not recalled, voluntarily versus involuntarily, during the diary period. The means for these four classes of pictures are presented in Table 2. A series of repeated measures ANOVAs each with two factors (corresponding to the recalled/not recalled and involuntary/voluntary distinctions) consistently showed substantial main effects of the recalled versus not recalled distinction (see Table 2), no effects of the voluntary versus involuntary distinction (all $ps > .2$) and no interactions (all $ps > .2$). Thus, pictures that were associated with more emotional response at encoding were more accessible for recall, irrespective of whether recall was voluntary or involuntary.

Pictures with a non-narrative content were more frequent among involuntary ($M = 1.61$) than voluntary memories ($M = 1.31$; $t(79) = 2.53$, $\eta^2 = .05$, $p < .05$, and vice versa for the complementary number of narrative pictures.

Retrieval qualities as a function of voluntary versus involuntary recall

Table 3 shows that the voluntary memories were rated significantly higher on *specificity*, *travel in time*, *vividness*, *details* and numerically higher on *colours* at the time of recall, whereas the differences went in the opposite direction for *self-relevance*, *bodily reaction*, *mood impact*, *valence*, and *intensity*—approaching significance in the case of mood impact, $t(63) = 1.86$, $\eta^2 = .05$, $p < .07$. The fact that the former cluster of variables followed a different pattern than the latter agrees with previous research showing that visual imagery and emotion are two partly independent components of episodic memory (Rubin, 2005, 2007).

Consistent with that view, the following composite scores were formed. The three variables measuring imagery (*vividness*, *colours*, *details*) showed a Cronbach's α of .89 and were averaged into a scale for *imagery*. *Bodily reaction*, *mood impact* (measured in absolute numbers), *valence* (absolute numbers), and *intensity* showed a Cronbach's α of .85 and were averaged into a scale for *emotion*. A repeated measures ANOVA with two factors (voluntary versus involuntary × imagery versus emotion) showed a significant interaction between the voluntary/involuntary distinction and the imagery/emotion distinction, $F(1, 63) = 9.12$, $MSE = 0.40$, $\eta_p^2 = .13$, $p < .005$. A Tukey HSD post hoc test showed that this interaction was due to the voluntary memories scoring higher than involuntary memories on imagery, whereas a non-significant difference in the opposite direction was found for the emotion measure.

TABLE 2
Encoding qualities

	Recalled				Not Recalled					
	Voluntary		Involuntary		Voluntary		Involuntary		Recalled/Not	
Encoding	*M*	*SD*	*M*	*SD*	*M*	*SD*	*M*	*SD*	$F(1, 51)$	η_p^2
Intensity	4.51	1.47	4.58	1.60	3.85	1.06	3.83	1.58	35.47***	.41
Valence	−1.59	0.87	−1.69	0.86	−1.20	0.41	−1.18	0.41	31.10***	.38
Dislike	4.69	1.51	4.91	1.50	4.15	1.07	4.10	1.07	23.28***	.31
Mood impact	−1.11	0.80	−1.20	0.89	−0.86	0.51	−0.83	0.47	16.54***	.25
Bodily react.	3.71	1.72	3.96	1.81	3.17	1.27	3.12	1.25	25.78***	.34
Self-relevance	2.13	1.32	2.29	1.37	1.88	0.75	1.86	0.75	7.79**	.13

Encoding qualities for pictures that were recalled versus not recalled voluntarily and involuntarily. **$p < .01$. ***$p < .0001$.

TABLE 3
Retrieval qualities for voluntary versus involuntary memories

	Voluntary		*Involuntary*			
Retrieval	*M*	*SD*	*M*	*SD*	*t*(63)	η^2
Specificity	5.63	1.39	4.98	1.68	3.10**	.13
Travel in time	3.50	1.55	3.10	1.47	2.83**	.11
Vividness	4.84	1.22	4.34	1.28	3.30**	.15
Colours	4.52	1.43	4.22	1.41	1.79	.05
Details	4.31	1.25	3.98	1.21	2.08*	.06
Self-relevance	2.47	1.33	2.62	1.42	−0.87	.01
Bodily reaction	2.50	1.36	2.64	1.45	−1.08	.02
Mood impact	−0.41	0.57	−0.56	0.66	1.86	.05
Valence	−0.76	0.83	−0.86	0.83	1.09	.02
Intensity	2.69	1.20	2.79	1.36	−0.87	.01

$^*p < .05$, $^{**}p < .01$.

Was this interaction related to the finding that non-narrative memories were more frequent among the involuntary memories? If so, we should expect memories for non-narrative pictures to have higher scores on emotion and memories for narrative pictures to have higher scores on imagery (irrespective of the voluntary/involuntary dimension). A repeated measures ANOVA with two factors (narrative versus non-narrative × imagery versus emotion) showed an interaction in the opposite direction, $F(1, 45) = 23.35$, $MSE = 0.29$, $\eta_p^2 = .34$, $p < .0001$. A Tukey HSD post hoc test showed that memories of the non-narrative pictures had higher scores on *imagery* than memories of the narrative pictures, whereas no difference was found for the emotion variable.

Memory qualities at the time of recall as a function of encoding qualities

In order to examine the relations between measures obtained at encoding and measures of memory qualities taken at recall, we first formed an emotional response composite variable, averaging for each participant the following five encoding variables: *intensity*, *valence* (absolute number), *bodily reaction*, *dislike*, and *mood impact* (absolute number). These variables were highly intercorrelated (*Average* $r = .78$) and showed a Cronbach's α of .92 (self-reference correlated weakly with the other encoding variables and was therefore not included in the composite variable). The new emotional response variable was found to correlate positively with the emotion composite score for recall, $r(297) = .58$, $p < .0001$), but not with the visual imagery composite score at recall, $r(297) = .08$, $p > .1$, contrary to the idea that strong emotional reaction at encoding is related to higher levels of visual imagery at recall (Brewin et al., 1996; Ehlers & Clark, 2000). This finding was confirmed in a series of multiple regression analyses that included self-reference as a predictor variable and dummy-coded subject variables to partial out subject variance (Cohen & Cohen, 1983; Thompson, Skowronski, Larsen, & Betz, 1996). and also in an analysis including voluntary/involuntary recall as a dichotomous dummy variable.

Individual differences

Results related to individual differences are shown in Table 4. The DES was systematically related to the memory qualities of the involuntary memories, whereas it was a significant predictor for only two of the measures for the voluntary memories. The VVIQ tended to show a reverse pattern: It was a significant predictor for three of the measures for voluntary memories, but did not show a systematic pattern with regards to memory qualities for the involuntary memories.

DISCUSSION

To our knowledge, this is the first time that involuntary versus voluntary memories have been related directly to ratings of emotions obtained during encoding, and also the first time

TABLE 4
Beta coefficients

	Voluntary					Involuntary				
Individual dif.	*Image*	*Emotion*	*Self*	*Travel*	*Specific*	*Image*	*Emotion*	*Self*	*Travel*	*Specific*
DES	0.15	0.30*	0.12	0.38**	0.02	0.39**	0.36*	0.39**	0.49**	0.27^
PCL	−0.08	−0.14	−0.08	−0.17	0.00	0.01	0.02	0.01	0.02	0.18
CES	−0.14	0.21	0.24	−0.00	−0.03	−0.03	0.10	0.14	0.10	0.00
STAI-T	0.29	0.27	−0.03	0.31*	0.09	−0.01	0.12	−0.19	−0.03	−0.12
STAI-S	−0.22	−0.19	−0.00	−0.04	−0.20	−0.35*	−0.01	0.14	−0.01	−0.30
VVIQ	0.20	0.27*	0.33*	0.30*	0.07	0.11	0.16	0.15	0.22	−0.13
R^2	0.13	0.25	0.17	0.31	0.03	0.21	0.23	0.25	0.34	0.13

β coefficients from multiple regression analyses predicting memory qualities with measures of individual differences ($N = 63$).
$^\wedge p < .06$. $*p < .05$. $**p < .01$.
DES = Dissociative Experience Scale; PCL = Post-traumatic Stress Disorder Checklist;
CES = Centrality of Event Scale; STAI-T = Trait Anxiety; STAI-S = State Anxiety;
VVIQ = Vividness of Visual Imagery Questionnaire (reversed here).

that phenomenological ratings of involuntary and voluntary memories for experimental stimuli have been compared. By comparing the ratings given during encoding for pictures recalled voluntarily versus involuntarily, the present study was able to examine the claim that involuntary recall, to a greater extent than voluntary recall, gives access to emotionally stressful information (e.g., Ehlers & Clark, 2000; Horowitz, 1986a, 1986b; van der Kolk & Fisler, 1995). In accordance with predictions generated from general memory theory, we found no differences between the voluntary and involuntary memories regarding the level of emotion associated with the remembered pictures at encoding: For both types of recall, pictures that were remembered had activated substantially more emotion at encoding than pictures that were not remembered.

Further, we found that pictures with a narrative content were more often recalled voluntarily than involuntarily. This finding supports the assumption that voluntary recall to a greater degree than involuntary recall involves a conceptually based retrieval strategy in which schema-generated search descriptions are used to generate more specific information (Berntsen, 1998; Berntsen & Hall, 2004; Conway & Playdell-Pearce, 2000). Likewise, the finding supports predictions based on clinical theories (e.g., Holmes et al., 2004).

By investigating records of memory qualities during recall, we found that voluntary memories scored higher than involuntary memories on measures of imagery vividness, whereas involuntary memories tended to score higher on measures of emotion—together showing a significant interaction between type of recall and memory qualities. This effect could not be explained by the differential narrative content of the two types of memories. The findings on visual imagery disagree with clinical theories assuming higher levels of visual imagery for involuntary than for voluntary memories (e.g., Brewin et al., 1996; Ehlers & Clark, 2000).

According to clinical theories (e.g., Brewin et al., 1996; Ehlcrs & Clark, 2000), cmotion ratings at encoding would be positively related to visual imagery during involuntary memory retrieval. We did not find support for this assumption. Emotion at encoding correlated only with emotion at recall and this pattern was uninfluenced by involuntary versus voluntary retrieval.

We found scores on the DES to be associated with both frequency and recollective qualities of the involuntary memories but only to a lesser extent with the recollective qualities of the voluntary memories. The VVIQ, on the other hand, was a predictor for several measures of recollective qualities for voluntary memories but not for involuntary memory quality. This dissociation provides some support for the supposition that involuntary and voluntary recall relies on separate or partly separate mechanisms.

Certain limitations should be considered when evaluating the present findings. First, to test whether the identified differences between involuntary and voluntary memories are specific to negatively valenced stimuli, positive and/or neutral pictures might have been included. However, by varying stimuli only along a dimension of negative emotional stress, we attempted to ensure uniform variations along the dimension of experienced emotional distress without confounding this dimension with other factors (such as distinctiveness, narrative content, or self-relevance) that might vary between negative, neutral, and positive conditions. Also, theories of the effect of emotion on memory processing focus on the arousal component as opposed to the valence component of emotional reactions. Emotional arousal is most reliably induced with negatively valenced material, motivating our choice of stimuli. However, future studies should include neutral and/or positive conditions to further examine the effect of emotional content on the two types of retrieval.

Second, future studies should be designed to specifically test the hypothesis of voluntary recall giving better access than involuntary recall to material with a narrative content, and to investigate the relationship between narrative content and memory vividness.

Third, it might be argued that reactions to aversive pictures cannot be generalised to real-life traumas or to the long-term reactions of PTSD patients. For example, PTSD patients clearly experience much more durable effects on memory than the ones shown here. This is a relevant discussion, which calls for future studies of voluntary and involuntary memories in specific trauma populations. However, the experimental procedure employed in the present study was motivated by previous experimental work on stressful intrusive memories in the clinical literature. Leading clinicians in the field of traumatic reactions have used "trauma analogue" aversive visual stimuli in experiments on intrusive memories, under the explicit assumption that reactions to such moderately stressful stimuli in healthy subjects capture general stress response mechanisms (e.g., Ehlers et al., 2006; Holmes et al., 2004; Horowitz, 1986a). Even if future studies should show that their work and the present findings are of limited relevance to specific trauma populations, the present work still adds important findings to the literature on stress reactions and intrusive memories in general.

Manuscript received 13 October 2006
Manuscript accepted 2 February 2007
First published online 16 May 2007

REFERENCES

American Psychiatric Association. (1994). *Diagnostic and statistic manual of mental disorders* (4th ed.). Washington, DC: American Psychiatric Association.

Arntz, A., de Groot, C., & Kindt, M. (2005). Emotional memory is perceptual. *Journal of Behavior Therapy and Experimental Psychiatry, 36*, 19–34.

Bernstein, E. M., & Putnam, F. W. (1986). Development, reliability, and validity of a dissociation scale. *Journal of Nervous and Mental Disease, 174*, 727–735.

Berntsen, D. (1998). Voluntary and involuntary access to autobiographical memory. *Memory, 6*, 113–141.

Berntsen, D. (2001). Involuntary memories of emotional events. Do memories of traumas and extremely happy events differ? *Applied Cognitive Psychology, 15*, 135–158.

Berntsen, D. (2007). Involuntary autobiographical memories: Speculations, findings and an attempt to integrate them. In J. Mace (Ed.), *Involuntary memory.* Oxford: Blackwell.

Berntsen, D., & Hall, N. M. (2004). The episodic nature of involuntary autobiographical memories. *Memory and Cognition, 32*, 789–803.

Berntsen, D., & Rubin, D. C. (2006). The centrality of event scale: A measure of integrating a trauma into one's identity and its relation to post-traumatic stress disorder symptoms. *Behaviour Research and Therapy, 44*, 219–231.

Berntsen, D., Willert, M., & Rubin, D. C. (2003). Splintered memories or vivid landmarks? Qualities and organisation of traumatic memories with and without PTSD. *Applied Cognitive Psychology, 17*, 675–693.

Blanchard, E. B., Jones-Alexander, J., Buckley, T. C., & Forneris, C. A. (1996). Psychometric properties of the PTSD Checklist (PCL). *Behaviour Research and Therapy, 34*, 669–673.

Bradley, M. M., Greenwald, M. K., Petry, M. C., & Lang, P. J. (1992). Remembering pictures: Pleasure and arousal in memory. *Journal of Experimental Psychology: Learning, Memory, and Cognition, 18*, 379–390.

Brewin, C. R., Dalgleish, T., & Joseph, S. (1996). A dual representation theory of post-traumatic stress disorder. *Psychological Review, 103*, 670–686.

Brewin, C. R., & Saunders, J. (2001). The effect of dissociation at encoding on intrusive memories for a stressful film. *British Journal of Medical Psychology, 74*, 467–472.

Cahill, L., & Alkire, M. T. (2003a). Epinephrine enhancement of human memory consolidation: Interaction with arousal at encoding. *Neurobiology of Learning and Memory, 79*, 194–198.

Cahill, L., Gorski, L., & Le, K. (2003b). Enhanced human memory consolidation with post-learning stress: Interaction with the degree of arousal at encoding. *Learning & Memory, 10*, 270–274.

Christianson, S-A. (Ed.). (1992). *The handbook of emotion and memory: Research and theory.* Hillsdale, NJ: Lawrence Erlbaum Associates Inc.

Cohen, J., & Cohen, P. (1983). *Applied multiple regression/correlation analysis for the behavioural sciences* (2nd ed.). Hillsdale, NJ: Lawrence Erlbaum Associates Inc.

Conway, M. A., & Pleydell-Pearce, C. W. (2000). The construction of autobiographical memories in the self-memory system. *Psychological Review, 107*, 261–288.

Cooper, B. S., Yuille, J. C., & Kennedy, M. A. (2002). Divergent perspectives in prostitutes' autobiographical memories: Trauma and dissociation. *Journal of Trauma & Dissociation, 3*, 75–95.

Davies, M. I., & Clark, D. M. (1998). Predictors of analogue post-traumatic intrusive cognitions. *Behavioral and Cognitive Psychotherapy, 26*, 303–314.

Dolcos, F., LaBar, K. S., & Cabeza, R. (2004). Interaction between the amygdala and the medial temporal lobe memory system predicts better memory for emotional events. *Neuron, 42*, 855–863.

Dolcos, F., LaBar, K. S., & Cabeza, R. (2005). Remembering one year later: Role of the amygdala and the medial temporal lobe memory system in retrieving emotional memories. *Proceedings of the National Academy of Sciences of the United States of America, 102*, 2626–2631.

Ehlers, A., & Clark, D. M. (2000). A cognitive model of post-traumatic stress disorder. *Behaviour Research and Therapy, 38*, 319–345.

Ehlers, A., Michael, T., Chen, Y. P., Payne, E., & Shan, S. (2006). Enhanced perceptual priming for neutral stimuli in a traumatic context: A pathway to intrusive memories? *Memory, 14*, 316–328.

Foa, E. B., & Riggs, D. S. (1995). Post-traumatic-stress-disorder following assault – Theoretical considerations and empirical findings. *Current Directions in Psychological Science, 4*, 61–65.

Foa, E. B., & Rothbaum, B. O. (1998). *Treating the trauma of rape: Cognitive-behavioral therapy of PTSD*. New York: Guilford Press.

Geday, J., Gjedde, A., Boldsen, A. S., & Kupers, R. (2003). Emotional valence modulates activity in the posterior fusiform gyrus and inferior medial prefrontal cortex in social perception. *Neuroimage, 18*, 675–684.

Geraerts, E., Kozaric-Kovacic, D., Merkelbach, H., Peraica, T., Jelicic, M., & Candel, I. (2007). Traumatic memories of war veterans: Not so special after all. *Consciousness and Cognition, 16*, 170–177.

Greenberg, D. L., & Rubin, D. C. (2003). The neuropsychology of autobiographical memory. *Cortex, 39*, 687–728.

Gross, J. J. (2001). Emotion regulation in adulthood: Timing is everything. *Current Directions in Psychological Science, 10*, 214–219.

Halligan, S. L., Clark, D. M., & Ehlers, A. (2002). Cognitive processing, memory, and the development of PTSD symptoms: Two experimental analogue studies. *Journal of Behavior Therapy and Experimental Psychiatry, 33*, 73–89.

Holmes, E. A., Brewin, C. R., & Hennessy, R. G. (2004). Trauma films, information processing, and intrusive memory development. *Journal of Experimental Psychology: General, 133*, 3–22.

Horowitz, M. J. (1975). Intrusive and repetitive thoughts after experimental stress: A summary. *Archives of General Psychiatry, 32*, 1457–1463.

Horowitz, M. J. (1986a). *Stress response syndromes* (2nd ed.). Northvale, NJ: Jason Aronson.

Horowitz, M. J. (1986b). Stress-response syndromes: A review of post-traumatic and adjustment disorders. *Hospital and Community Psychiatry, 37*, 241–249.

Lang, P. J., Bradley, M. M., & Cuthbert, B. (1995). *The international affective picture system (IAPS)*. The Center for Research in Psychophysiology, University of Florida, Gainesville, FL, USA.

Marks, D. F. (1989). Construct validity of the Vividness of Visual Imagery Questionnaire. *Perceptual and Motor Skills, 69*, 459–465.

McGaugh, J. L. (2004). The amygdala modulates the consolidation of memories of emotionally arousing experiences. *Annual Review of Neuroscience, 27*, 1–28.

Porter, S., & Birt, A. R. (2001). Is traumatic memory special? A comparison of traumatic memory characteristics with memory for other emotional life experiences. *Applied Cognitive Psychology, 15*, S101–S117.

Rubin, D. C. (2005). A basic-systems approach to autobiographical memory. *Current Directions in Psychological Science, 14*, 79–83.

Rubin, D. C. (2007). The basic-systems model of episodic memory. *Perspectives on Psychological Science, 1*, 277–311.

Rubin, D. C., Feldman, M. D., & Beckham, J. C. (2004). Reliving, emotions, and fragmentation in the autobiographical memories of veterans diagnosed with PTSD. *Applied Cognitive Psychology, 18*, 17–35.

Spielberger, C., Gorsuch, R., Lushene, R., Vagg, P., & Jacobs, G. (1983). *Manual for the State-Trait Anxiety Inventory (form Y self-evaluation questionnaire)*. Palo Alto, CA: Consulting Psychologists Press.

Thompson, T. C., Skowronski, J. S., Larsen, S. F., & Betz, A. L. (1996). *Autobiographical memory: Remembering what and remembering when*. Hillsdale, NJ: Lawrence Erlbaum Associates Inc.

van der Kolk, B. A., & Fisler, R. (1995). Dissociation and the fragmentary nature of traumatic memories – Overview and exploratory study. *Journal of Traumatic Stress, 8*, 505–525.

Weathers, F. W., Litz, B. T., Herman, D. S., Huska, J. A., & Keane, T. M. (1994). *The PTSD checklist: Reliability, validity, and diagnostic utility*. Paper presented at the annual meeting of the International Society for Traumatic Stress Studies, San Antonio, TX, USA.

Wegner, D. M. (1989). *White bears and other unwanted thoughts: Suppression, obsession, and the psychology of mental control*. New York: Penguin Press.

MEMORY, 2008, 16 (1), 58–75
Psychology Press
Taylor & Francis Group

Trauma and memory: Effects of post-event misinformation, retrieval order, and retention interval

Pedro M. Paz-Alonso and Gail S. Goodman
University of California, Davis, CA, USA

The present study concerned effects of misinformation, retrieval order, and retention interval on eyewitness memory for a traumatic event (a vivid murder). Relations between misinformation acceptance and compliance were also examined. The classic three-stage misinformation paradigm (Loftus, 1979) was employed, with a multi-component recognition test added. Either immediately or 2 weeks after viewing a distressing film, 232 adults read a narrative (misleading or control) about the murder and then took a recognition test that tapped memory for central and peripheral details. Test-item order either matched the chronology of the film or was randomly determined. Significant misinformation effects were obtained. Moreover, control participants were more accurate in response to questions about central than peripheral information; however, this was not so for misinformed participants. Sequential but not random retrieval order resulted in a higher proportion of correct responses for central as opposed to peripheral misinformation questions. Compliance was significantly related to misinformation effects. Delay increased participants' suggestibility, impaired memory accuracy, and produced higher confidence ratings for misinformed participants compared to controls. Findings indicate that even for a highly negative event, adults' memory is not immune to inaccuracies and suggestive influences.

In the present experiment, adults' memory and suggestibility about details of a highly negative emotional event (a vivid murder) were investigated. Although adult eyewitness memory has been studied for years by means of the misinformation effect paradigm (e.g., Loftus, 1979; Loftus, Schooler, & Wagenaar, 1985), relatively few experiments have examined such effects for traumatic acts, such as murder.

Post-event misinformation often leads to errors in adults' memory reports (e.g., Loftus, Miller, & Burns, 1978). Although this phenomenon is widely accepted, controversy exists regarding the generalisability of the findings to traumatic material. Moreover, theoretical explanations for the misinformation effect are debated, as are the appropriate methodological procedures to uncover potential memory distortion (e.g., Brainerd & Reyna, 1998; Lindsay & Johnson, 2000; McCloskey & Zaragoza, 1985). These debates are particularly heated when memory for highly negative events is at issue.

In this paper we first review effects of negative emotion on memory and suggestibility. Second, we discuss theories of the misinformation effect as relevant to the present study, specifically theories that emphasise storage interference or social influence. Third, we describe the main methodological approaches employed to test these theories. Fourth, effects of delay on eyewitness memory and suggestibility are reviewed. Finally, the present study is described.

Address correspondence to: Dr Pedro M. Paz-Alonso, Department of Psychology, University of California, 1 Shields Avenue, Davis, CA 95616, USA. E-mail: ppazalonso@ucdavis.edu

This study was funded by a pre-doctoral grant to the first author from the Program in Research Training (Department of Education, Universities, and Research) of the Basque Government. We thank Izaskun Ibabe, Arantza Gorostiaga, and Shannon Riley for their support.

http://www.psypress.com/memory DOI:10.1080/09658210701363146

MEMORY AND SUGGESTIBILITY FOR EMOTIONAL STIMULI

Contradictory data exist about the accuracy of memory for highly negative emotional stimuli. Christianson (1992) concluded that, when an event is highly distressing, the main stressor is especially well remembered, due to heightened preattentive processes and greater rehearsal and consolidation. Many field and laboratory studies confirm that central information that elicits a strongly negative emotional reaction tends to be retained with particular accuracy (e.g., Berntsen & Thomsen, 2005; Christianson & Hübinette, 1993; Fivush, Sales, Goldberg, Bahrick, & Parker, 2004). Studies of amygdala activation support such findings (e.g., LeDoux, 2000; McGaugh & Cahill, 2003; Phelps, 2006). In contrast, regarding distressing events, details peripheral to the main stressor are often less accurately remembered than are comparable details in neutral events (e.g., Brown, 2003; Burke, Heuer, & Reisberg, 1992; Loftus & Burns, 1982; see Goodman & Paz-Alonso, 2006, for review). However, Deffenbacher, Bornstein, Penrod, and McGorty (2004) contend that such studies have not included events of a sufficiently traumatic (e.g., life-threatening) nature to produce a defensive reaction that can interfere with memory. Thus, particularly accurate memory for central versus peripheral information within distressing events is not necessarily a stable or generally accepted phenomenon (e.g., Wessel, van der Kooy, & Merckelbach, 2000). Also, valence and arousal may correspond to distinct neural processes. Nevertheless, information with negative valence, even if non-arousing, is better remembered than neutral information (e.g., Kensinger & Corkin, 2004a, 2004b).

The debate about distress and memory is relevant to the question of whether stressful and traumatic events are somehow immune to the misinformation effect. For example, if central features of highly negative events are retained with particular accuracy, they may be resistant to post-event misinformation, especially after short delays. The relatively few studies that have examined the effects of misinformation on memory for such events tend to deal with public incidents about which there is likely to have been considerable discussion and media attention. For example, Nourkova, Bernstein, and Loftus (2004) examined whether it is possible to experimentally contaminate memory for truly traumatic events. In their study, Russian adults reported on their memories for either the 1999 terrorist bombings on apartment buildings in Moscow or the 2001 attacks on the World Trade Center in New York. Across 6 months, participants recalled the events on two separate occasions. Prior to the second recall, the researchers provided misinformation indicating that participants had seen a wounded animal in the attacks and had mentioned it in their original memory reports. Approximately 13% of the Moscow group accepted the false suggestion. This group rated the personal significance of the Moscow bombings as lower than did those who resisted the suggestion. No one in the World Trade Center group was convinced by the (perhaps less plausible) suggestion (Pezdek & Hodge, 1999; Scoboria, Mazzoni, Kirsch, & Relyea, 2004). Although these findings support the notion that traumatic memories are at times malleable, the post-misinformation question was arguably more about participants' previous memory report than the traumatic events per se. In related research, Crombag, Wagenaar, and van Koppen (1996) examined whether misinformation would lead adults to believe that they had witnessed something they had only heard reports about from others. Adults were asked whether they saw a TV film of the crashing of an El Al Boeing 747 on apartment buildings in Amsterdam and how long it took for the fire to start after the crash. Although no TV film exists of the crash, a high percentage of adults (55%) confirmed that they had seen the crash on TV (see also Ost et al.'s study in this special issue of *Memory*).

In a misinformation effect study that did not deal with public events, Porter, Spencer, and Birt (2003) presented adults with highly positive or highly negative emotional photographs, or neutral photographs, followed an hour later by misinformation. A recall test was then administered. There were no significant differences between emotion conditions on correct recall despite misinformation. Misinformation had a stronger adverse effect on memory for misleading peripheral than central details. However, for false information about whether an animal had been in the scene, negative emotion was associated with increased susceptibility to suggestion.

These studies indicate that memory for distressing events can be contaminated by misinformation. However, most of the studies have not differentiated between central and peripheral information. In the Porter et al. study, which made this differentiation, the effect of emotion on the overall misinformation effect was not significant for central or peripheral information. Given the mixed results and relative paucity of research, further study is justified.

THEORIES OF MISINFORMATION EFFECTS

Theoretical accounts of the misinformation effect have been based on memory for neutral to mildly stressful stimuli. It is unclear if theory needs to be expanded or changed to take into consideration traumatic memories, given their purported special memory status. Loftus initially proposed the trace alteration theory, specifically that post-event misinformation overwrites original memory traces (e.g., Loftus, 1975). According to this theory, misleading post-event information generates an automatic updating of memory that results in a permanent loss of the original information.

Subsequent research and theory have resulted in alternative interpretations of the misinformation effect. For example, more recent theories rely on notions of trace strength (e.g., Brainerd & Reyna, 1998; Marche, 1999), memory coexistence and retrieval blocking (e.g., Bekerian & Bowers, 1983), associative activation theory (Ayers & Reder, 1998), source monitoring (e.g., Lindsay & Johnson, 1989), and social-demand characteristics (e.g., McCloskey & Zaragoza, 1985).

Memory coexistence/retrieval blocking and retrieval order

Of particular relevance to the present study is the memory coexistence/retrieval blocking notion. According to this idea, memories of the original information and the misinformation co-exist. However, retrieval of the original memory trace is often blocked by retrieval of the more recent and thus potentially stronger misinformation trace, rendering the original information inaccessible or non-retrievable, at least under certain circumstances (e.g., Bekerian & Bowers, 1983). In formulating this theory, Bekerian and Bowers (1983) noted that in Loftus's misinformation effect studies, recognition test items were presented in random order as opposed to in an order that matched the chronology of the stimulus event's unfolding. In Bekerian and Bowers' study, if the test reinstated the original event order, misinformed adults performed equivalently on subsequent memory tests compared to controls who had not been exposed to misinformation. This finding suggested, contrary to trace alteration theory, that the original memory was still accessible. However, later research revealed that chronological retrieval order does not guarantee elimination of the misinformation effect (see Bowers & Bekerian, 1984).

In the present study, effects of retrieval order were examined for memory and suggestibility about a highly negative event. As far as we know, such order effects have not been previously investigated in a misinformation study that concerned highly negative material. It is possible that memory for traumatic material, being potentially more fragmented (e.g., van der Hart, Bolt, & van der Kolk, 2005), is especially likely to require the support afforded by correct chronological order of retrieval cues. Furthermore, consistent with Christianson's (1992) conclusions, retrieval order might differentially support retrieval of original memories for central details of distressing events, which are retained relatively well, but might not as fully benefit original memory for peripheral details, which might be too weak in memory to profit.

Social demands and compliance

The social-demand approach highlights the contribution of social-related factors to false information acceptance. For example, an important part of McCloskey and Zaragoza's (1985) argument against trace alteration theory was that, in the standard misinformation paradigm, misleading suggestions may be reported because of social-demand characteristics that promote participants' compliance with the interviewer-provided suggestion (see also Cassel, Roebers, & Bjorklund, 1996; Roebers & Schneider, 2000).

Nevertheless, rarely addressed in former research is the relation between compliance—defined as responding "yes" to a specific misleading question (e.g., Shapiro, Blackford, & Chiung-Fen, 2005)—and misinformation effects. Eyewitness memory researchers have shown that young children's memory reports are often more adversely affected than those of older children and adults due to compliance with misleading questions (e.g., Goodman &

Reed, 1986; Roebers, Schwarz, & Neumann, 2005). However, adults are also sensitive to the social-demand characteristics inherent in misinformation studies (e.g., Gabbert, Memon, Allan, & Wright, 2004; Smith & Ellsworth, 1987). In many such studies it is not possible to separate, on the one hand, response bias or compliance to misleading questions from, on the other hand, memory failures (Roebers & Schneider, 2000). It has been argued, however, that due to the different mechanisms involved, compliance and misinformation effects should be distinguished (Davies, Flin, & Baxter, 1986; Gee & Pipe, 1995).

In the present experiment, after adults viewed the murder, misinformed participants read a misleading narrative either immediately or 2 weeks later. The same day, at the retrieval phase, the adults were asked questions related to the previously presented misinformation (i.e., *misinformation questions* to measure misinformation effects), as well as questions that included new false information that was not presented previously (i.e., *specific-misleading questions* to measure compliance). In this way, false information acceptance was assessed separately in terms of misinformation effects and compliance. Specific questions that did not include false information (i.e., *specific-correct questions*) were also included to serve as a measure of recognition memory accuracy. Moreover, the test items were presented in a random order or in an order that chronologically followed that of the film. As a result, effects of retrieval context could be examined.

METHODOLOGICAL APPROACHES

In her initial studies, Loftus examined the misinformation effect using what is often termed "the standard procedure", in which a two-alternative forced-choice recognition test was presented. The two alternatives were the original and suggested items (Loftus & Palmer, 1974; Loftus et al., 1978). However, the standard procedure has been criticised as a pure measure of memory malleability because it may involve social-demand factors and hinder source memory (Johnson, Hashtroudi, & Lindsay, 1993; McCloskey & Zaragoza, 1985).

McCloskey and Zaragoza (1985) proposed the modified procedure, which attempts to control for demand characteristics in the testing situation. In the modified procedure, participants choose between the original item and a new foil item (an item neither previously presented nor suggested). The modified procedure typically produces a reduction in the magnitude of the misinformation effect, and at times even eliminates it (Payne, Toglia, & Anastasi, 1994; Zaragoza, 1987, 1991). However, it has been argued that exclusion of the suggested item at test reduces sensitivity to memory impairment (e.g., Tversky & Tuchin, 1989).

To address criticisms regarding the modified procedure, researchers devised recognition tests that included the original, suggested, and new foil items (e.g., Gobbo, 2000, Experiment 1; Pezdek & Roe, 1995). Inclusion of such alternatives facilitates assessment of whether misinformed participants simply forgot the original items, and thus gave an equal proportion of incorrect responses to the suggested and the new foil items, or whether participants' memory reports were specifically misled by the items suggested in the narrative (Pezdek & Roe, 1995; Tversky & Tuchin, 1989).

Finally, regarding methodology, forced-choice and yes/no recognition tests are commonly used in misinformation studies. This is problematic in the sense that a "don't know" alternative is typically unavailable. Therefore, the forced-choice and yes/no recognition tests may produce a particularly high proportion of commission errors and an overestimation of the magnitude of the misinformation effect, especially when the suggested item is included within the response alternatives (McCloskey & Zaragoza, 1985). Few misinformation studies have included an explicit "don't know" response alternative (e.g., Higham, 1998; Roebers & Schneider, 2000). Yet permitting participants to say "I don't know" when they are uncertain is a critical factor for memory accuracy (Koriat & Goldsmith, 1994). Moreover, in forensic contexts, witnesses can answer "don't know", which is clearly preferable to an incorrect answer (e.g., Wells & Bradfield, 1998).

For the present study, to tap misinformation effects, a recognition test was constructed that included the following response options: correct, misled, new foil, and don't know. Inclusion of the four response options provides an especially robust test for identifying the effects of post-event misinformation on memory.

DELAY, EYEWITNESS MEMORY, AND SUGGESTIBILITY

Delay plays an important role in acceptance of misleading suggestions, regardless of whether such acceptance is studied by means of the classic misinformation paradigm or via compliance-oriented procedures (e.g., Goodman, Bottoms, Schwartz-Kenney, & Rudy, 1991; Roebers & Schneider, 2000). In misinformation effect studies, acceptance of false information is also influenced by the time interval between event presentation and misinformation (Loftus, 1979), perhaps because the susceptibility of verbatim memories to retroactive interference increases as such memories are forgotten (Reyna, 1995). In studies producing suggestibility effects, including ones that rely on Loftus's standard paradigm, misinformation is usually delayed until a day or more after the acquisition session (e.g., Pezdek & Roe, 1995; Roberts, Lamb, & Sternberg, 1999).

In several misinformation studies using newer testing procedures, researchers have varied retention interval. For example, when the modified procedure is employed, misinformation effects are evident at short retention intervals but primarily for peripheral information (e.g., Belli, Lindsay, Gales, & McCarthy, 1994; Schwartz-Kenney & Goodman, 1999; Wright & Stroud, 1998). For central features of the original event, such effects are evident at long retention intervals (Ackil & Zaragoza, 1995; Belli, Windschitl, McCarthy, & Winfrey, 1992). Thus, delay and information centrality may interact in affecting misinformation effects.

Delay is also an important variable in assessing the effects of arousal on memory and suggestibility (Belli et al., 1992, 1994; Burke et al., 1992). Some research has shown negative effects of arousal on adults' memory at short retention intervals (e.g., Clifford & Scott, 1978; Loftus & Burns, 1982). However, in these studies, memory for peripheral information was largely tested. With longer retention intervals, arousal has tended to improve memory for event information (e.g., Christianson, 1984; Heuer & Reisberg, 1990). Few studies have examined the influence of retention interval on the misinformation effect for central versus peripheral details of vivid negative emotional events.

EYEWITNESS CONFIDENCE AND MEMORY FOR EMOTIONAL STIMULI

Confidence judgements regarding memory are generally considered to reflect an individual's internal subjective estimation of the accuracy of his or her recollection (e.g., Roebers, 2002). An individual's confidence judgements may provide a match (i.e., "calibration") or not (i.e., "miscalibration") with his or her accuracy. An example of calibration is that adult participants tend to appropriately give higher confidence ratings after correct than incorrect responses (e.g., Nolan & Markham, 1998; Robinson, Johnson, & Robertson, 2000). Miscalibration in the confidence–accuracy relation may be due to either underconfidence, when an individual's confidence is lower than his or her accuracy, or overconfidence, when an individual's confidence is higher than his or her accuracy (Koriat, Lichtenstein, & Fischhoff, 1980; Roebers, 2002). Confidence is an important factor affecting perceptions of witness credibility (e.g., Goodman et al., 1998; Lindsay, 1994; Penrod & Cutler, 1995). Nevertheless, confidence–accuracy relations are typically weak to moderate (e.g., Wells, 1993; but see Robinson & Johnson, 1996). Some authors have suggested that eyewitness accuracy and confidence might be based on different cognitive mechanisms (Busey, Tunnicliff, Loftus, & Loftus, 2000), and that therefore confidence may be governed in part by factors that are unrelated to accuracy (Wells, Olson, & Charman, 2002).

Inaccurate witnesses are at times as confident in their responses as accurate witnesses (e.g., Sporer, Penrod, Read, & Cutler, 1995). And, of special relevance, misinformed witnesses may exhibit overconfidence in their false reports, producing higher confidence in their incorrect responses compared to the responses of witnesses who did not receive false post-event information (e.g., Weingardt, Leonesio, & Loftus, 1994), or may show as much confidence in their correct responses as in their incorrect answers to misleading questions (e.g., Loftus, Donders, Hoffman, & Schooler, 1989). Using the misinformation effect paradigm, and similar retention intervals to the ones used in the present study (immediate vs 2 week), Mudd and Govern (2004) found that over time (2 weeks) participants exposed to misinformation became more confident of their memories, whereas control participants became less confident. However, in that study the correct versus incorrect nature of participants' specific responses was not examined. Moreover, misinformation research on confidence and memory has generally not concerned memory for highly distressing material. Given notions that central information is retained particularly well after a negatively arousing event, misinformation effects may be hard to obtain for such information and, relatedly, confidence in memory may be higher for central than peripheral information. To date, there is almost no empirical evidence about eyewitness confidence for central versus peripheral true and false details regarding emotional events.

THE PRESENT STUDY

The present study examined effects of misleading information, retrieval order, and retention interval on adults' memory accuracy, suggestibility, and confidence judgements for central versus peripheral information about a highly negative emotional film. Despite contradictory results in the empirical literature about memory and emotion, the traumatic nature of some witnessed events may play a critical role in eyewitness memory.

For the present experiment, participants viewed the emotional film and then after a varying retention interval were either presented with a misleading narrative or a non-misleading narrative. A recognition test with misinformation, specific-misleading, and specific-correct questions followed immediately after the narrative. All recognition test questions included four response alternatives: one correct, two incorrect, and a "don't know" answer option (see Table 1). The test questions were presented in either a retrieval order that matched the order of events in the film or in a random order.

Overall, the experimental design conformed to a 2 (Condition: misinformed, control) × 2 (Retrieval Order: sequential, random) × 2 (Retention Interval: immediate, 2-week) × 2 (Centrality: central, peripheral) mixed factorial with the latter factor varied within subjects. We examined: (1) The misinformation effect, that is, performance on 10 misinformation questions that referred to false post-event details included in the narrative; (2) compliance in relation to 20 specific-misleading questions that included inaccurate information not presented previously; (3) performance on 30 specific-correct questions that included correct information about the film; and, (4) confidence judgements regarding recognition accuracy.

According to previous research findings, a number of predictions were advanced. First, consistent with classic misinformation effects, misinformed versus control participants were expected to show higher acceptance of misinformation (e.g., Loftus, 1979). Thus, misinformation effects were predicted despite the emotional nature of the witnessed event.

TABLE 1
Question type examples and response alternatives

	Misinformation effects	*Compliance*	*Recognition accuracy*
Question type	*Misinformation questions* ($n = 10$) Concerned false details embedded in the misinformation narrative	*Specific-misleading questions* ($n = 20$) Included inaccurate information (not presented previously in the film or narrative)	*Specific-correct questions* ($n = 30$) Included correct information about the film
Example	*"Without trying to escape, did the person die?"* (when in fact the person tried to escape)	*"Did the car continue moving while the taxi driver was being hit by the murderer?"* (when in fact the car was stopped)	*"Was it during the daytime when the person died?"* (when in fact it was during daytime)
Recognition test: Response alternatives	*Misled*: "Yes." *New foil*: "No, the person shouts for help." *Correct*: "No." *"Don't Know"*	*Compliance:* "Yes." *Incorrect*: "No, no one was being hit." *Correct*: "No, it stopped." *"Don't Know"*	*Correct:* "Yes." *Incorrect*: "No, it was at dusk" *Incorrect*: "No, it was at dawn." *"Don't Know"*

Question type examples and response alternatives used in the recognition test to examine misinformation effects, compliance, and recognition accuracy.

Second, according to previous studies testing the memory coexistence/retrieval blocking hypothesis, and consistent with the encoding specificity principle (Tulving & Thomson, 1973), it was expected that use of a sequential order that matched the chronology of the film's unfolding as opposed to a random order would increase (although not entirely eliminate) resistance to misinformation (e.g., Bekerian & Bowers, 1983). For misled participants, retrieval order was expected to be particularly helpful for retrieval of original central information, consistent with Christianson's (1992) theory about distress and memory.

Third, associations between answers to specific-misleading questions and misinformation effects were investigated. In a previous study we found that compliance with inaccurate information embedded in specific-misleading questions was positively associated with misinformation acceptance, especially after a delay (Paz-Alonso, Goodman, & Ibabe, 2007). In the present study, we expected to replicate that finding, especially regarding peripheral information, given that social-demand effects may be particularly operative when memory traces are weakened.

Fourth, it was predicted that delay would increase misinformation effects, as well as compliance (e.g., Belli et al., 1992; Roebers & Schneider, 2000), and would decrease the accuracy of performance on specific questions generally (e.g., Brainerd, Reyna, Howe, & Kingma, 1990; Roebers & Schneider, 2000).

Fifth, according to Christianson (1992), negative emotionally arousing information bolsters memory especially in relation to central compared to peripheral or irrelevant details. If so, eyewitness memory should be better for central than peripheral details, because the former should be less subject to misinformation effects and because people should be less compliant concerning specific-misleading questions about central than peripheral information. In addition, adults should be particularly accurate in their responses to specific-correct questions for central information. Also, it is reasonable to expect that peripheral compared to central information would be more prone to decay with delay (e.g., Cassel et al., 1996).

Sixth, based on evidence from misinformation studies, it was expected that misinformed eyewitnesses would exhibit as much confidence in their correct responses as in their misled answers to misinformation questions (e.g., Loftus et al., 1989). Similarly, at the 2-week delay, misinformed versus control participants should show higher confidence in their misled responses (Mudd & Govern, 2004). Finally, higher confidence judgements were expected after correct compared to incorrect answers to specific-correct questions (e.g., Robinson et al., 2000).

METHOD

Participants

In total, 232 undergraduate students (195 females) from the University of the Basque Country, ranging in age from 18 to 46 years old ($M = 20.28$, $SD = 5.12$), participated for course credit.

Materials

An event (murder) extracted from Kieslowski's film "Decalogue V: A short film about killing" (Chutkowski & Kieslowski, 1988) was selected. The event's total length was 5 minutes 40 seconds, and it contained three parts: introduction (1 minute), emotional focus (3 minutes 40 seconds), and end (1 minute). During the introduction, a young man and a taxi driver are travelling in a taxi cab. The car stops at a pedestrian pathway and several children accompanied by an adult cross the road. The car proceeds to the outskirts of town. Suddenly, the young man starts strangling the taxi driver with a rope, and then repeatedly hits the taxi driver with a club. After the murder, the young man remains in the car listening to the radio.

Two versions of a *narrative text* about the film were constructed. This narrative included either 10 false post-event details (e.g., "The taxi driver did not try to escape and ends up dying", when in fact he tried to escape) that constituted the misinformation for participants assigned to the misinformed condition, or no false post-event details (e.g., "The taxi driver ends up dying"; control condition).

To assess event memory, a *multiple choice recognition test* with 60 specific questions was constructed. Half of the questions were specific-correct (e.g., "Was the young man's hair light and wavy?", when in fact his hair was light and wavy); 20 questions from the remaining half were specific-misleading (e.g., "Were the children wearing school uniforms?", when in fact they did not wear uniforms). The remaining 10 were misinformation questions and concerned the same 10 false items that were included in the misleading narrative (e.g., "Did the taxi driver die without attempting to escape?"). The 60 questions were either randomly intermixed or presented in a sequential order matching that of the film. Each question contained four answer options: one correct, two incorrect, and a "don't know" alternative. Of the 60 recognition test questions, 30 had a correct response option of "yes" and 30 had a correct response option of "no".

To avoid response bias, order of the correct and incorrect alternatives was counterbalanced across test questions, except that the "don't know" alternative always appeared last. Moreover, for 20 questions (e.g., "Does the taxi driver refuse to turn when his client asks him to?"), two incorrect response options were provided, one that indicated "yes" and another that indicated "no" (e.g., "Yes, he continued on a straight path" and "No, no one asked him to turn", respectively). For another 20 questions (e.g., "Did any of the people who appeared in the film look happy?"), two different incorrect "yes" response options were provided (e.g., "Yes, one person" and "Yes, several people"). Finally, for another 20 questions (e.g., "During the film, could several rows of buildings be seen?"), two different "no" incorrect response options were provided (e.g., "No, only one building could be seen" and "No"). Right after responding to each question, participants rated their response confidence on a 5-point Likert scale (0 = not sure at all to 4 = totally sure).

Finally, centrality was defined based on Ibabe and Sporer's (2004) critical event criteria (i.e., central details were defined as those that occurred during the critical event and/or that were related to the event's main characters). Based on this definition, 30 of the 60 recognition test questions tapped central information, and the remaining tapped peripheral information. The number of central and peripheral questions was equally distributed within misinformation (i.e., 5 central, 5 peripheral), specific-misleading (i.e., 10 central, 10 peripheral), and specific-correct questions (i.e., 15 central, 15 peripheral).[1]

Procedure

Participants were randomly assigned to experimental conditions, with 28 to 30 participants per condition. They watched the film in small groups (one to three individuals) without being informed of the study's purpose (e.g., that it concerned memory). First, participants were warned that some film scenes might cause discomfort; they were invited to leave the room if they felt uncomfortable while viewing the film (no one left the room). Following the film, participants were asked if they had seen it before or knew of it; none so indicated. They then completed two ratings regarding the film's valence ("How unpleasant was it to watch?" with 1 = not at all unpleasant and 7 = very unpleasant; $M = 5.59$, $SD = 1.17$), and arousing nature ("Did you feel uneasy while watching it?" with 1 = not at all uneasy and 7 = very uneasy; $M = 4.87$, $SD = 1.36$). A 5- to 7-minute filler task of answering questions about general knowledge was administered. Then either immediately after or 2 weeks later, participants read the narrative (misleading or control). Following the narrative and before the recognition test, they completed a similar filler task (5–7 minutes). Next, the recognition test was administered, before which participants were repeatedly instructed to answer all of the questions only on the basis of what they saw in the film. Immediately after answering each of the recognition questions, participants were instructed to rate their response confidence—except when they responded "don't know". Participants were asked not to discuss the film or study procedure with others.

RESULTS

A series of 2 (Condition: misinformed vs control) × 2 (Retrieval Order: sequential vs random) × 2 (Retention Interval: immediate vs 2-week) × 2 (Centrality: central vs peripheral) mixed analyses of variance (ANOVAs) was conducted, with centrality as the only within-subject factor. All significant effects are reported. Eta-square values (η^2) are provided as estimators of effect sizes.

[1] For the present study, the designation of central and peripheral questions using the Ibabe and Sporer critical event criteria was made in collaboration with Ibabe.

Misinformation effects

Answers to the 10 misinformation questions were scored as misled (i.e., the answer that was consistent with the narrative's false information), new foil (i.e., the answer representing the new alternative), correct (i.e., the answer that represented the information presented in the film), and "don't know" responses.

Analysis of proportion of misled responses revealed significant main effects for condition and retention interval, $Fs(1, 224) \geq 8.09$, $MSEs = .07$, $ps < .01$, $\eta^2 \geq .04$. Participants in the misinformed condition selected a higher proportion of misled alternatives ($M = .45$, $SD = .25$) than did those in the control condition ($M = .17$, $SD = .21$), replicating the well-known misinformation effect. Compared to participants at the immediate retention interval, participants at the 2-week delay produced a higher proportion of misled responses (see Table 2). However, the condition main effect was qualified by a significant Condition × Centrality interaction, $F(1, 224) = 7.50$, $MSE = .03$, $p < .01$, $\eta^2 = .03$. This interaction was due to the misinformed participants' higher proportion of misled responses to central misinformation questions ($M = .49$, $SD = .30$) than to peripheral ones ($M = .42$, $SD = .28$), $F(1, 115) = 6.95$, $MSE = .04$, $p < .05$, $\eta^2 = .06$ (simple effects). In contrast, for control participants, there was no significant simple effect for the proportion of misled responses to central versus peripheral misinformation questions. Thus, although the intended misinformation effect was evident, surprisingly, misinformed but not control participants exhibited higher acceptation of central compared to peripheral misinformation.

In the analyses of correct responses to misinformation questions, main effects of condition and retention interval were also significant, $Fs(1, 224) \geq 9.15$, $MSEs = .07$, $ps < .01$, $\eta^2 s \geq .04$. Control participants ($M = .41$, $SD = .18$) produced a higher proportion of correct responses to misinformation questions compared to misinformed participants ($M = .25$, $SD = .20$). And participants at the immediate versus 2-week interval were more correct responding to misinformation questions. Moreover, there was a significant Retrieval order × Centrality interaction, $F(1, 224) = 4.89$, $MSE = .03$, $p < .05$, $\eta^2 = .02$ (see Figure 1). Of interest, sequential retrieval order produced a higher proportion of correct responses to central misinformation questions than to peripheral ones, $F(1, 115) = 8.65$, $MSE = .03$, $p < .01$, $\eta^2 = .07$ (simple effects). This difference was not significant when correct responses to central versus peripheral misinformation questions were examined for the random retrieval order condition.

The ANOVA for the new foil items showed a significant main effect of retention interval, $F(1, 224) = 10.54$, $MSE = .02$, $p < .01$, $\eta^2 = .05$. Participants assigned to the 2-week versus immediate condition produced a higher proportion of new foil responses. Finally, the analysis of proportion of "don't know" responses revealed significant main effects for condition and centrality, $Fs(1, 224) \geq 16.51$, $MSEs \geq .03$, $ps < .001$, $\eta^2 s \geq .07$. Misinformed participants exhibited a lower proportion of "don't know" responses ($M = .22$, $SD = .19$) than did control participants ($M = .34$, $SD = .19$). Peripheral misinformation questions were answered with a higher proportion of "don't know" responses than central ones. Also, a significant Retention Interval × Centrality interaction emerged, $F(1, 224) = 16.51$, $MSE = .03$, $p < .001$, $\eta^2 = .07$. Simple effects analyses revealed that participants produced a higher proportion of "don't know" responses to central misinformation questions at the immediate compared to 2-week test, $F(1, 230) = 7.67$, $MSE = .05$, $p < .01$, $\eta^2 = .03$. This difference was not significant for peripheral misinformation questions. Also, at the 2-week delay participants selected a higher proportion of "don't know" responses to peripheral misinformation questions than to central ones, $F(1, 111) = 20.29$, $MSE = .03$, $p < .001$, $\eta^2 = .16$. There were no significant differences at the immediate interval for "don't know" responses to central and peripheral misinformation questions.

In summary, we found misinformation effects for a highly negative emotional event, even with the inclusion of a "don't know" alternative. Delay negatively influenced performance across the memory measures and increased the proportion of "don't know" responses to peripheral misinformation. Of importance, sequential retrieval order facilitated participants' resistance to central compared to peripheral misinformation. However, surprisingly, misinformed participants showed a higher acceptance of central false details compared to peripheral ones.

TABLE 2
Responses by retention interval and centrality

	Immediate			*Two-week*			*Total*		
	Central	*Peripheral*	*Means*	*Central*	*Peripheral*	*Means*	*Central*	*Peripheral*	*Means*
Misinformation Questions									
Misled responses	.28 (.29)	.27 (.24)	.27 (.23)	.36 (.30)	.33 (.27)	.35 (.25)	.32 (.29)	.30 (.26)	.31 (.24)
New foil responses	.06 (.11)	.05 (.11)	.06 (.07)	.11 (.15)	.08 (.12)	.09 (.10)	.08 (.13)	.06 (.12)	.08 (.09)
Correct responses	.37 (.22)	.37 (.25)	.37 (.19)	.32 (.25)	.27 (.24)	.30 (.21)	.35 (.24)	.32 (.25)	.33 (.20)
"Don't know" responses	.29 (.22)	.31 (.25)	.30 (.20)	.21 (.21)	.32 (.26)	.26 (.20)	.25 (.22)	.31 (.25)	.28 (.20)
Specific-misleading Questions									
Compliance responses	.09 (.08)	.17 (.12)	.13 (.07)	.13 (.12)	.19 (.12)	.16 (.09)	.11 (.10)	.18 (.12)	.15 (.08)
Incorrect responses	.16 (.11)	.21 (.13)	.19 (.09)	.20 (.14)	.25 (.14)	.22 (.10)	.18 (.13)	.23 (.13)	.20 (.10)
Correct responses	.66 (.15)	.58 (.15)	.62 (.11)	.58 (.18)	.37 (.19)	.48 (.15)	.62 (.17)	.48 (.20)	.55 (.15)
"Don't know" responses	.17 (.14)	.21 (.14)	.19 (.12)	.23 (.15)	.38 (.19)	.30 (.14)	.20 (.14)	.29 (.19)	.25 (.14)
Specific-correct Questions									
Correct responses	.72 (.11)	.48 (.15)	.60 (.11)	.60 (.13)	.34 (.15)	.47 (.11)	.66 (.13)	.42 (.17)	.54 (.13)
Incorrect responses	.22 (.10)	.27 (.13)	.24 (.10)	.27 (.11)	.32 (.13)	.30 (.09)	.25 (.11)	.29 (.13)	.27 (.10)
"Don't know" responses	.06 (.07)	.25 (.14)	.16 (.09)	.13 (.10)	.33 (.15)	.23 (.11)	.09 (.09)	.29 (.15)	.19 (.11)

Mean proportions of responses to misinformation, specific-misleading, and specific-correct questions by retention interval and centrality.

Standard deviations in parentheses. Columns for specific-misleading questions sum over 1.00 because compliance responses included "yes" answers, and incorrect responses included both "yes" and "no" answers.

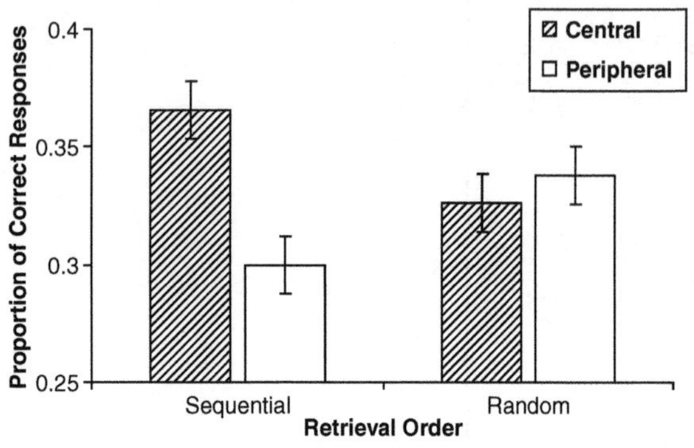

Figure 1. Mean proportions of correct responses to misinformation questions as a function of centrality and retrieval order.

Participants' compliance and performance on specific-misleading questions

Responses to the 20 specific-misleading questions were scored as proportion compliance (i.e., incorrect responses of "yes"), incorrect (i.e., "yes" and "no" incorrect responses), correct, and "don't know". A series of ANOVAs, as described earlier, was conducted for each of these dependent measures (Table 2). The analysis of compliance responses as well as of incorrect responses overall showed significant main effects for retention interval and centrality, $Fs(1, 224) \geq 8.98$, $MSEs \geq .01$, $ps < .01$, $\eta^2s \geq .04$. Compared to participants tested immediately, participants tested after a 2-week delay were more incorrect overall, including by complying more with the inaccurate information contained in specific-misleading questions. Peripheral specific-misleading questions produced a higher proportion of incorrect and compliance responses than central ones.

In analyses of correct and "don't know" responses, the significant main effects of retention interval and centrality were subsumed by a significant Retention Interval × Centrality interaction, $Fs(1, 224) \geq 20.75$, $MSEs \geq .02$, $ps < .001$, $\eta^2s \geq .09$. Participants tested after 2 weeks were more correct and produce fewer "don't know" responses to central than to peripheral specific-misleading questions, $Fs(1, 111) \geq 68.07$, $MSEs \geq .02$, $ps < .001$, $\eta^2 \geq .38$ (simple effects). These differences were non-significant for the immediate condition. Moreover, peripheral specific-misleading questions were answered with a higher proportion of "don't know" responses at the 2-week delay than immediately, $F(1, 230) = 57.66$, $MSE = .03, p < .001, \eta^2 = .20$ (simple effects).

In summary, at the 2-week but not at the immediate test, participants were more correct and produced a lower proportion of "don't know" responses to central compared to peripheral specific-misleading questions.

Performance on specific-correct questions

Participants' performance on 30 specific-correct questions was examined to assess recognition accuracy. These questions did not contain false information, and they were not related to the misinformation contained in the narrative text. Therefore, participants' responses to the two incorrect alternatives were scored together as proportion of incorrect responses. Three mixed-model ANOVAs, as described earlier, were computed separately for proportion of correct, incorrect, and "don't know" responses (Table 2).

Analyses revealed significant main effects of retention interval and centrality across all three dependent measures. Compared to those tested at the 2-week delay, participants tested immediately showed a higher proportion of correct responses, and a lower proportion of both incorrect and "don't know" responses, $Fs(1, 224) \geq 22.46$, $MSEs = .02$, $ps < .001$, $\eta^2s \geq .09$. Also, specific-correct questions related to central versus peripheral information resulted in a higher proportion of correct responses, and a lower proportion of incorrect and "don't know" responses, $F(1, 224) \geq 26.03$, $MSEs = .01$, $ps < .001$, $\eta^2s \geq .10$. Thus, recognition accuracy declined with delay, and memory was superior for central information.

Correlations between participants' performance on misinformation questions and specific-misleading questions

Correlational analyses were performed to examine whether, as predicted, adults' responses to misinformation questions and specific-misleading questions were significantly related. A correlation between errors to the misinformation questions and compliance with specific-misleading questions was particularly expected for peripheral false information and at the 2-week delay. Half of the participants were exposed to the misinformation narrative, and thus could be included in these analyses ($N = 116$).

The predicted correlations were substantial, and the pattern of associations is enlightening. Overall, when centrality is not considered, the correlation between compliant responses to specific-misleading questions (i.e., compliance) and misled responses to misinformation questions (i.e., misinformation effect) was significant, $r = .24$, $p < .01$. Compliance with specific-misleading questions predicted suggestibility in terms of the misinformation effect. However, this significant correlation was primarily the result of adults' performance on peripheral questions, $r = .25$, $p < .01$. Thus, certain participants showed a *general* tendency to accept false information (misinformation presented in the narrative and in specific-misleading questions), especially in regard to peripheral details. There was also a significant positive association between incorrect responses to specific-misleading questions and misled responses to misinformation questions, $r = .18$, $p < .05$, as well as a negative association between correct responses to specific-misleading questions and misled responses to misinformation questions, $r = -.16$, $p < .05$. And, again, these associations were primarily driven by adults' performance on peripheral false details, $rs \geq |.19|$, $ps < .05$.

There was a significant positive correlation between correct responses to specific-misleading questions and correct responses to misinformation questions overall, $r = .26$, $p < .01$, as well as for peripheral false information, $r = .35$, $p < .01$. Adults who could resist inaccurate information contained in specific-misleading questions were also more resistant to misinformation. And, consistent with this finding, there was a significant negative correlation between "don't know" responses to specific-misleading questions and correct responses to misinformation questions overall, $r = -.31$, $p < .01$, as well as for central, $r = -.18$, $p < .05$, and peripheral false information, $r = -.32$, $p < .01$. Thus, responding "don't know" to false information embedded in specific-misleading questions was negatively associated with responding correctly to misinformation questions.

The correlations between saying "don't know" to the specific-misleading and misinformation questions were especially high and significant, indicating that some participants had a tendency to say "don't know". And, of special interest, responding "don't know" to misinformation questions was negatively associated with errors in responding to specific-misleading questions (i.e., compliant and incorrect responses). All these associations were significant overall, $rs \geq -.34$, $ps < .01$, as well as for central and peripheral false information, $rs \geq -.23$, $ps < .01$.

Finally, when retention interval was considered, the mentioned overall significant correlation between errors to the misinformation questions and compliance responses to specific-misleading questions was only found at the 2-week delay, $r\ (56) = .24$, $p < .05$, not at the immediate delay, $r\ (60) = .20$, $p > .05$. Thus with time, presumably as memory faded, a subset of adults showed a general false information acceptance tendency. Also, it should be noted that participants' incorrect responses to specific-correct questions overall were not significantly related to participants' misled responses to misinformation questions, $r = -.06$, $p < .05$, and not to participants' compliance responses to specific-misleading questions, $r = .17$, $p < .05$, respectively.

Confidence judgements

To examine participants' confidence in their misled responses to misinformation questions, an identical mixed model ANOVA to those described earlier was conducted. It should be noted that this analysis included participants who provided at least one misled response and made a corresponding confidence rating for that response ($N = 134$). Also, to examine participants' ability to monitor and evaluate their own retrieval process, paired *t*-test comparisons were conducted between individuals' mean confidence to errors (i.e., misled, compliance, and incorrect responses to specific-misleading and specific-correct questions) and to correct responses within the different type of questions analysed (i.e., misinformation, specific-misleading, and specific-correct).

The mixed model ANOVA for mean confidence ratings for misled responses revealed a significant main effect of centrality, $F(1, 126) = 5.54$, $MSE = .52$, $p < .05$, $\eta^2 = .04$. Participants showed higher confidence in their misled responses to central ($M = 3.95$, $SD = .90$) than to peripheral misinformation questions ($M = 3.72$, $SD = .99$). Moreover, there was a significant Condition × Retention Interval interaction, $F(1, 126) = 9.20$, $MSE = 1.19$, $p < .01$, $\eta^2 = .07$. As predicted, at the 2-week delay, misinformed participants ($M = 4.12$, $SD = .62$), compared to controls ($M = 3.58$, $SD = .93$), exhibited higher confidence in their misled responses, $F(1, 102) = 12.23$, $MSE = .62$, $p < .01$, $\eta^2 = .11$ (simple effects). This difference between misinformed and control participants' mean confidence ratings was not significant at the immediate retention interval.

Our prediction that participants would show as much confidence in their misled responses as in their correct answers to misinformation questions was confirmed. Participants' mean confidence ratings for correct ($M = 3.69$, $SD = .74$) versus misled ($M = 3.76$, $SD = .87$) responses to misinformation questions did not differ significantly, $t(187) = .95$, $p > .05$. Also, when only misinformed participants were included in this comparison ($N = 92$), there was not a significant difference in confidence judgements for correct ($M = 3.69$, $SD = .85$) compared to misled ($M = 3.88$, $SD = .76$) responses, $t(91) = 1.81$, $p > .05$ (e.g., Loftus et al., 1989). This result suggests that participants were not able to differentiate true from false responses in their metamemory judgements, which is consistent with the memory impairment hypotheses of the misinformation effect.

We also conducted analyses to examine if there were significant differences in confidence judgements for compliance and incorrect or correct responses to specific-misleading questions. Participants showed significantly higher mean confidence ratings for correct ($M = 3.93$, $SD = .52$) compared to compliance ($M = 3.66$, $SD = .76$) or incorrect ($M = 3.56$, $SD = .80$) responses, $ts(212\text{-}220) \geq 5.80$, $ps < .001$. Thus, although a subset of participants showed compliance by answering "yes" when confronted with inaccurate information embedded in specific-misleading questions, the participants' metamemory judgements about the correctness of their responses differed between their hits and false alarms; specifically, their confidence was higher for hits. Finally, as expected, participants' mean confidence ratings were significantly higher for correct responses ($M = 4.16$, $SD = .42$) than for incorrect responses ($M = 3.64$, $SD = .53$) to specific-correct questions, $t(231) = 16.92$, $p < .001$.

DISCUSSION

This study investigated adult eyewitness memory and suggestibility regarding a murder shown in a highly emotional film. Our primary goals were to examine associations between two suggestibility measures (i.e., misinformation effects and compliance) and to investigate recognition accuracy and suggestibility for central and peripheral details as a function of retrieval order and retention interval. Also, we examined adults' confidence judgements about the correctness of their responses to questions tapping misinformation effects, compliance, and recognition accuracy.

Misinformation effects, retrieval order, and compliance

Consistent with our first prediction, significant misinformation effects were obtained (e.g., Loftus, 1979; Loftus et al., 1978). Misinformed participants responded more incorrectly than did controls to misinformation questions related to details that were falsely described in the misleading narrative. Of interest, and in keeping with our second prediction, sequential retrieval order produced more correct responses; however, this finding was restricted to central misinformation questions. The effect of retrieval order was consistent with Christianson's (1992) proposal that central information about a stressful event is particularly well retained. As such, the correct retrieval order perhaps supported retrieval of the original memory for central information to the extent that it partly overcame the misinformation effect. The retrieval order effect was also consistent with the encoding specificity principle, which states that episodic memory is improved when information available at encoding is also available at retrieval (Tulving & Thomson, 1973). Thus, use of a sequential retrieval order that provided contextual cues regarding encoding information facilitated correct responses for central information about the act of murder.

However, also in accordance with our second prediction, the use of a sequential retrieval order as opposed to a random order did not eliminate misinformation effects. Bekerian and Bowers (1983) proposed that, although retrieval of the original memory trace can be blocked by retrieval of the potentially stronger misinformation trace, correct chronological retrieval order supports memory of the original information. Such support may be particularly needed for retrieval of highly emotional material, which might be stored in fragmented but vivid form (van der Hart et al., 2005). However, the fact that misinformation effects still existed despite correct chronological order could indicate true memory malleability or insufficient cues to retrieve the original (perhaps fragmentary) memory.

Also of importance, misinformation effects were robust even with the explicit option of responding "don't know". This response alternative was intended to control for guessing and also for possible source-monitoring conflicts between the original and suggested information (Higham, 1998). However, misinformed eyewitnesses compared to control participants produced a lower proportion of "don't know" responses to misinformation questions.

An additional finding of special relevance was that participants overall were equally confident about the correctness of their misled and correct responses. This "miscalibration" suggests that participants were not able to differentiate true from false information and possibly that they were not aware of the misinformation, which is consistent with the memory impairment hypotheses. Can we therefore conclude that misinformation impaired/interfered with memory of the original information? Probably not because results also showed positive associations between compliance and misinformation effects, indicating that misinformed participants who complied with the false information contained in specific-misleading questions also tended to be suggestible in terms of the misinformation effect. Also, positive associations were consistent across correct and "don't know" responses. Thus, eyewitnesses who resisted inaccurate information in, or responded "don't know" to, specific-misleading questions also showed higher resistance to accepting misinformation. Of importance, it should be noted that significant correlations were not obtained between incorrect responses on the misinformation questions and incorrect responses to the specific-correct questions, which argues against the notion that poor memory was responsible for the significant correlations between the compliance and misinformation responses (see also Coxon & Valentine, 1997). These associations highlight that even when trying to reduce social-demand influences and response bias, misinformation effects in this study were likely due to some extent to social-related factors.

Additionally, although a subset of participants showed compliance by answering "yes" when confronted with inaccurate information embedded in specific-misleading questions, the participants' metamemory judgements about the correctness of their responses to these questions differed between their hits and false alarms; specifically, their confidence was higher for hits. Thus, in contrast to the pattern for misinformation questions, the pattern for specific-misleading questions suggests that participants' errors may be mainly explained by conscious acquiescence or acceptance of the inaccurate information rather than by memory change or alteration. Of special interest is that this social influence on participants' suggestibility occurred with a methodological approach that incorporated some of the common features involved in applied eyewitness settings (e.g., a highly negative emotional event, the option to respond "don't know").

Effects of delay on eyewitness suggestibility and memory

One consistent finding was the effect of delay on memory and suggestibility. Misinformation effects, compliance, and errors to specific-misleading and specific-correct questions increased significantly with delay (e.g., Loftus, 1979). For example, consistent with results of previous studies, as memory faded witnesses tended to be more prone to accept misinformation and comply with specific-misleading questions (e.g., Belli et al., 1992; Reyna, 1995; Roberts et al., 1999). Delay appears to weaken the original memory trace so as to produce larger compliance and misinformation effects (e.g., Brainerd & Reyna, 1995), or so as to facilitate a higher alteration or interference of original memory by misinformation (e.g., Loftus, Levidow, & Duensing, 1992). The fact that positive associations between compliance and misinformation effects were primarily found at the 2-week delay also suggests that with delay misinformation effects may then be particularly due to social factors that more potently operate when memory is weak (Paz-Alonso et al., 2007). Moreover, with delay, misinformed versus control participants became more confident of their false memories (Mudd & Govern, 2004). Possibly, as memory faded, misinformed participants' reliance on the more recent misinformation also produced greater confidence in the correctness of their misled responses.

Centrality and eyewitness memory and suggestibility

The present study confirmed that eyewitness memory performance was better for central than for peripheral information. Delay negatively affected memory for peripheral information, which is consistent with previous findings that peripheral information is particularly prone to decay (e.g., Cassel et al., 1996). In the present study, memory for a non-emotional comparison film was not tested, and the possible effects of valence and arousal were not examined separately. Nevertheless, participants' ratings indicated that the film was unpleasant to view, producing a certain degree of uneasiness. Our results are consistent with research showing that negative emotionally arousing information enhances memory especially in relation to central information (e.g., Burke et al., 1992; Christianson, 1992; Wagenaar & Groeneweg, 1990). Although the unequal gender distribution in the sample may have affected our results (e.g., in terms of mean reactivity), the film's negative nature seemed generally to produce expected centrality results.

Of importance, the one exception concerned the fact that misinformed participants (but not controls) endorsed more misled responses to central than to peripheral misinformation questions. Misinformed participants' greater misinformation acceptance of central compared to peripheral information could be an artifact of the centrality definition utilised (i.e., critical event criteria; Ibabe & Sporer, 2004; Paz-Alonso et al., 2007), or it could be a verifiable finding. In the latter case, this result might be explained by the influence of both cognitive and social factors. Specifically, it is possible that misinformed participants remembered the misleading central information from the narrative better than they remembered the peripheral misleading information. As a result, the central misinformation might have been more accessible to memory (a cognitive factor). Moreover, when deciding how to respond on the recognition test, social factors might have further led some participants to err on central misinformation. Given the findings of "implanted memory" studies, in which, under certain conditions, adults and children can be led to report entirely fictitious events that never actually occurred (e.g., Ghetti & Alexander, 2004; Hyman, Husband, & Billings, 1995; Loftus & Pickrell, 1995), it should be no surprise that central information can be subject to misinformation effects. That said, the misinformation in our study did not concern the most central action in the film—that a man was murdered.

Finally, in a similar vein, eyewitnesses who selected the misinformation option (i.e., misled response) on the misinformation questions were more confident about their responses to central than to peripheral false details. This parallel finding, in relation to the misinformation effects analyses, may also be attributable to the higher salience of central compared to peripheral false details, supporting possible cognitive influences on misinformation acceptance.

Conclusion

Few studies have examined misinformation effects for highly negative events and fewer still have investigated relations between misinformation acceptance and compliance. Our findings confirm misinformation effects for an emotional film concerning a murder and point to both cognitive and social factors as contributing to misinformation phenomena. Reinstatement at test of the original event's order (i.e., sequential order) did not eliminate misinformation effects. However, sequential order resulted in significantly more correct responses to central than to peripheral misinformation details, whereas this difference was not significant when a random order was used at test. Of special theoretical and applied relevance, compared to control participants, eyewitnesses who received misinformation after a 2-week delay exhibited overconfidence in their false memories. Adults' memory for highly negative events is not immune to inaccuracies and suggestive influences.

Manuscript received 12 December 2006
Manuscript accepted 20 March 2007
First published online 17 May 2007

REFERENCES

Ackil, J. K., & Zaragoza, M. S. (1995). Developmental differences in eyewitness suggestibility and memory for source. *Journal of Experimental Child Psychology, 60*, 57–83.

Ayers, M. S., & Reder, L. M. (1998). A theoretical review of the misinformation effect: Predictions from an activation-based memory model. *Psychonomic Bulletin & Review*, *5*, 1–21.

Bekerian, D. A., & Bowers, J. M. (1983). Eyewitness testimony: Were we misled? *Journal of Experimental Psychology: Learning, Memory, and Cognition*, *9*, 139–145.

Belli, R. F., Lindsay, D. S., Gales, M. S., & McCarthy, T. T. (1994). Memory impairment and source misattribution in postevent misinformation experiments with short retention intervals. *Memory & Cognition*, *22*, 40–54.

Belli, R. F., Windschitl, P. D., McCarthy, T. T., & Winfrey, S. E. (1992). Detecting memory impairment with a modified test procedure: Manipulating retention interval with centrally presented event items. *Journal of Experimental Psychology: Learning, Memory, and Cognition*, *18*, 356–367.

Berntsen, D., & Thomsen, D. K. (2005). Personal memories for remote historical events: Accuracy and clarity of flashbulb memories related to World War II. *Journal of Experimental Psychology: General*, *134*, 242–257.

Bowers, J. M., & Bekerian, D. A. (1984). When will postevent information distort eyewitness testimony? *Journal of Applied Psychology*, *69*, 466–472.

Brainerd, C. J., & Reyna, V. F. (1995). Learning rate, learning opportunities, and the development of forgetting. *Developmental Psychology*, *31*, 251–263.

Brainerd, C. J., & Reyna, V. F. (1998). Fuzzy-trace theory and children's false memory. *Journal of Experimental Child Psychology*, *71*, 81–129.

Brainerd, C. J., Reyna, V. F., Howe, M. L., & Kingma, J. (1990). The development of forgetting and reminiscence. *Monographs of the Society for Research in Child Development*, *55*, 1–113.

Brown, J. M. (2003). Eyewitness memory for arousing events: Putting things into context. *Applied Cognitive Psychology*, *17*, 93–106.

Burke, A., Heuer, F., & Reisberg, D. (1992). Remembering emotional events. *Memory & Cognition*, *20*, 277–290.

Busey, T. A., Tunnicliff, J., Loftus, G. R., & Loftus, E. F. (2000). Accounts of the confidence–accuracy relation in recognition memory. *Psychonomic Bulletin & Review*, *7*, 26–48.

Cassel, W. S., Roebers, C. M., & Bjorklund, D. F. (1996). Developmental patterns of eyewitness responses to repeated and increasingly suggestive questions. *Journal of Experimental Child Psychology*, *61*, 116–133.

Christianson, S. Å. (1984). The relationship between induced emotional arousal and amnesia. *Scandinavian Journal of Psychology*, *25*, 147–160.

Christianson, S. Å. (1992). Emotional stress and eyewitness memory: A critical review. *Psychological Bulletin*, *112*, 284–309.

Christianson, S. Å., & Hübinette, B. (1993). Hands up: A study of witnesses' emotional reactions and memories associated with bank robberies. *Applied Cognitive Psychology*, *7*, 365–379.

Clifford, B. R., & Scott, J. (1978). Individual and situational factors in eyewitness testimony. *Journal of Applied Psychology*, *3*, 352–359.

Chutkowski, R., [Producer] & Kieslowski, K. [Director] (1988). *Decalogue V: A short film about killing* [motion picture]. Poland: Tor Films.

Coxon, P., & Valentine, T. (1997). The effects of the age of the witness on the accuracy and suggestibility of their testimony. *Applied Cognitive Psychology*, *11*, 415–430.

Crombag, H. F. M., Wagenaar, W. A., & van Koppen, P. J. (1996). Crashing memories and the problem of "source monitoring". *Applied Cognitive Psychology*, *10*, 95–104.

Davies, G. M., Flin, R. H., & Baxter, J. S. (1986). The child witness. *Howard Journal*, *25*, 81–99.

Deffenbacher, K. A., Bornstein, B. H., Penrod, S. D., & McGorty, E. K. (2004). A meta-analytic review of the effects of high stress on eyewitness memory. *Law and Human Behavior*, *28*, 687–706.

Fivush, R., Sales, J. M., Goldberg, A., Bahrick, L., & Parker, J. (2004). Weathering the storm: Children's long-term recall of hurricane Andrew. *Memory*, *12*, 104–118.

Gabbert, F., Memon, A., Allan, K., & Wright, D. B. (2004). Say it to my face: Examining the effects of socially encountered misinformation. *Legal and Criminological Psychology*, *9*, 215–227.

Gee, S., & Pipe, M. E. (1995). Helping children to remember: The influence of object cues on children's accounts of a real event. *Developmental Psychology*, *31*, 746–758.

Ghetti, S., & Alexander, K. W. (2004). "If it happened, I would remember it": Strategic use of event memorability in the rejection of false autobiographical events. *Child Development*, *75*, 542–561.

Gobbo, C. (2000). Assessing the effects of misinformation on children's recall: How and when makes a difference. *Applied Cognitive Psychology*, *14*, 163–182.

Goodman, G. S., Bottoms, B. L., Schwartz-Kenney, B. M., & Rudy, L. (1991). Children's testimony about a stressful event: Improving children's reports. *Journal of Narrative and Life History*, *1*, 69–99.

Goodman, G. S., & Paz-Alonso, P. M. (2006). Trauma and memory: Normal versus special memory mechanisms. In B. Uttl, N. Ohta, & A. L. Siegenthaler (Eds.), *Memory and emotion: Interdisciplinary perspectives*. Oxford, UK: Blackwell Publishing.

Goodman, G. S., & Reed, R. S. (1986). Age differences in eyewitness testimony. *Law and Human Behavior*, *10*, 317–332.

Goodman, G. S., Tobey, A. E., Batterman-Faunce, J. M., Orcutt, H., Thomas, S., Shapiro, C., et al. (1998). Face-to-face confrontation: Effects of closed-circuit technology on children's eyewitness testimony and jurors' decisions. *Law and Human Behavior*, *22*, 165–203.

Heuer, F., & Reisberg, D. (1990). Vivid memories of emotional events: The accuracy of remembered minutiae. *Memory & Cognition*, *18*, 496–506.

Higham, P. A. (1998). Believing details known to have been suggested. *British Journal of Psychology*, *89*, 265–283.

Hyman, I. E. Jr., Husband, T. H., & Billings, F. J. (1995). False memories of childhood experiences. *Applied Cognitive Psychology*, *9*, 181–197.

Ibabe, I., & Sporer, S. L. (2004). How you ask is what you get: On the influence of question form on accuracy and confidence. *Applied Cognitive Psychology, 18*, 1–16.

Johnson, M. K., Hashtroudi, S., & Lindsay, D. S. (1993). Source monitoring. *Psychological Bulletin, 114*, 3–28.

Kensinger, E. A., & Corkin, S. (2004a). Two routes to emotional memory: Distinct neural processes for valence and arousal. *Proceedings of the National Academy of Sciences, 101*, 3310–3315.

Kensinger, E. A., & Corkin, S. (2004b). Memory enhancement for emotional words: Are emotional words more vividly remembered than neutral words. *Memory & Cognition, 31*, 1169–1180.

Koriat, A., & Goldsmith, M. (1994). Memory in naturalistic and laboratory contexts: Distinguishing the accuracy-oriented and quantity-oriented approaches to memory assessment. *Journal of Experimental Psychology: General, 123*, 297–315.

Koriat, A., Lichtenstein, S., & Fischhoff, B. (1980). Reasons for confidence. *Journal of Experimental Psychology: Human Learning and Memory, 6*, 107–118.

LeDoux, J. (2000). Emotion circuits in the brain. *Annual Review of Neuroscience, 23*, 155–184.

Lindsay, D. S. (1994). Memory source monitoring and eyewitness testimony. In D. F. Ross, J. D. Read, & M. P. Toglia (Eds.), *Adult eyewitness testimony: Current trends and developments* (pp. 27–55). Cambridge, UK: Cambridge University Press.

Lindsay, D. S., & Johnson, M. K. (1989). The eyewitness suggestibility effect and memory for source. *Memory & Cognition, 17*, 349–358.

Lindsay, D. S., & Johnson, M. K. (2000). False memory and the source monitoring framework. Reply to Reyna and Lloyd (1997). *Learning and Individual Differences, 12*, 145–161.

Loftus, E. F. (1975). Leading questions and the eyewitness report. *Cognitive Psychology, 7*, 560–572.

Loftus, E. F. (1979). *Eyewitness testimony.* Cambridge, MA: Harvard University Press.

Loftus, E. F., & Burns, T. E. (1982). Mental shock can produce retrograde amnesia. *Memory & Cognition, 10*, 318–323.

Loftus, E. F., Donders, K., Hoffman, H. G., & Schooler, J. W. (1989). Creating new memories that are quickly acceded and confidently held. *Memory & Cognition, 17*, 607–616.

Loftus, E. F., Levidow, B., & Duensing, S. (1992). Who remembers best? Individual differences in memory for events that occurred in a science museum. *Applied Cognitive Psychology, 6*, 93–107.

Loftus, E. F., Miller, D. G., & Burns, H. J. (1978). Semantic integration of verbal information into a visual memory. *Journal of Experimental Psychology: Human Learning and Memory, 4*, 19–31.

Loftus, E. F., & Palmer, J. C. (1974). Reconstruction of automobile destruction: An example of the interaction between language and memory. *Journal of Verbal Learning and Verbal Behavior, 13*, 585–589.

Loftus, E. F., & Pickrell, J. E. (1995). The formation of false memories. *Psychiatric Annals, 25*, 720–725.

Loftus, E. F., Schooler, J. W., & Wagenaar, W. A. (1985). The fate of memory: Comment on McCloskey & Zaragoza. *Journal of Experimental Psychology: General, 114*, 375–380.

Marche, T. A. (1999). Memory strength affects reporting of misinformation. *Journal of Experimental Child Psychology, 73*, 45–71.

McCloskey, M., & Zaragoza, M. S. (1985). Misleading postevent information and memory for events: Arguments and evidence against memory impairment hypotheses. *Journal of Experimental Psychology: General, 117*, 171–181.

McGaugh, J. L., & Cahill, L. (2003). Emotion and memory: Central and peripheral contributions. In R. J. Davidson, K. R. Scherer, & H. H. Goldsmith (Eds.), *Handbook of affective sciences* (pp. 93–116). New York: Oxford University Press.

Mudd, K., & Govern, J. M. (2004). Conformity to misinformation and time delay negatively affect eyewitness confidence and accuracy. *North American Journal of Psychology, 6*, 227–238.

Nolan, J., & Markham, R. (1998). The accuracy–confidence relationship in an eyewitness task: Anxiety as a modifier. *Applied Cognitive Psychology, 12*, 43–54.

Nourkova, V., Bernstein, D. M., & Loftus, E. F. (2004). Altering traumatic memory. *Cognition & Emotion, 18*, 575–585.

Ost, J., Granhag, P.-A., Udell, J., Roos, E., & Hjelmsater, E. R. (2007). Familiarity breeds distortion: The effects of media exposure on false reports concerning media coverage of the terrorist attacks in London on 7 July 2005. *Memory, 16*, 76–85.

Payne, D. G., Toglia, M. P., & Anastasi, J. S. (1994). Recognition performance level and the magnitude of the misinformation effect in eyewitness memory. *Psychonomic Bulletin & Review, 1*, 376–382.

Paz-Alonso, P. M., Goodman, G. S., & Ibabe, I. (2007). *Adult eyewitness memory and compliance: Effects of post-event misinformation on memory for a negative event.* Manuscript submitted for publication.

Penrod, S., & Cutler, B. (1995). Witness confidence and witness accuracy: Assessing their forensic relation. *Psychology, Public Policy, and Law, 1*, 817–845.

Pezdek, K., & Hodge, D. (1999). Planting false childhood memories in children: The role of event plausibility. *Child Development, 70*, 887–895.

Pezdek, K., & Roe, C. (1995). The effect of memory trace strength on suggestibility. *Journal of Experimental Child Psychology, 60*, 116–128.

Phelps, E. (2006). Emotion and cognition: Insights from studies of the human amygdala. *Annual Review of Psychology, 57*, 27–53.

Porter, S., Spencer, L., & Birt, A. R. (2003). Blinded by emotion? Effect of the emotionality of a scene on susceptibility to false memories. *Canadian Journal of Behavioral Science, 35*, 165–175.

Reyna, V. F. (1995). Interference effects in memory and reasoning: A fuzzy-trace theory and analysis. In F. N. Dempster & C. J. Brainerd (Eds.), *Interference and inhibition in cognition* (pp. 29–59). San Diego, CA: Academic Press.

Roberts, K. P., Lamb, M. E., & Sternberg, K. J. (1999). Effects of the timing of postevent information on

preschoolers' memories of an event. *Applied Cognitive Psychology, 13*, 541–559.
Robinson, M. D., & Johnson, J. T. (1996). Recall memory, recognition memory, and the eyewitness confidence–accuracy correlation. *Journal of Applied Psychology, 81*, 587–594.
Robinson, M. D., Johnson, J. T., & Robertson, D. A. (2000). Process versus content in eyewitness metamemory monitoring. *Journal of Experimental Psychology: Applied, 6*, 207–221.
Roebers, C. M. (2002). Confidence judgements in children's and adults' event recall and suggestibility. *Developmental Psychology, 38*, 1052–1067.
Roebers, C. M., & Schneider, W. (2000). The impact of misleading questions on eyewitness memory in children and adults. *Applied Cognitive Psychology, 14*, 509–526.
Roebers, C. M., Schwarz, S., & Neumann, R. (2005). Social influence and children's event recall and suggestibility. *European Journal of Developmental Psychology, 2*, 47–69.
Schwartz-Kenney, B. M., & Goodman, G. S. (1999). Children's memory of a naturalistic event following misinformation. *Applied Developmental Science, 3*, 34–46.
Scoboria, A., Mazzoni, G., Kirsch, I., & Relyea, M. (2004). Plausibility and belief in autobiographical memory. *Applied Cognitive Psychology, 18*, 791–807.
Shapiro, L. R., Blackford, C., & Chiung-Fen, C. (2005). Eyewitness memory for a simulated misdemeanor crime: The role of age and temperament in suggestibility. *Applied Cognitive Psychology, 19*, 489–506.
Smith, V. L., & Ellsworth, P. C. (1987). The social psychology of eyewitness accuracy: Misleading questions and communicator expertise. *Journal of Applied Psychology, 72*, 294–300.
Sporer, S., Penrod, S., Read, D., & Cutler, B. L. (1995). Choosing, confidence, and accuracy: A meta-analysis of the confidence-accuracy relation in eyewitness identification studies. *Psychological Bulletin, 118*, 315–327.
Tulving, E., & Thomson, D. M. (1973). Encoding specificity and retrieval processes in episodic memory. *Psychological Review, 80*, 352–373.
Tversky, B., & Tuchin, M. (1989). A reconciliation of the evidence on eyewitness testimony: Comments on McCloskey & Zaragoza. *Journal of Experimental Psychology: General, 118*, 86–91.
van der Hart, O., Bolt, H., & van der Kolk, B. A. (2005). Memory fragmentation in dissociative identity disorder. *Journal of Trauma & Dissociation, 6*, 55–70.
Wagenaar, W. A., & Groeneweg, J. (1990). The memory of concentration camp survivors. *Applied Cognitive Psychology, 4*, 77–88.
Weingardt, K. R., Leonesio, R. J., & Loftus, E. F. (1994). Viewing eyewitness research from a metacognitive perspective. In J. Metcalfe & A. P. Shimamura (Eds.), *Metacognition: Knowing about knowing* (pp. 157–184). Cambridge, MA: The MIT Press.
Wells, G. L. (1993). What do we know about eyewitness identification? *American Psychologist, 48*, 553–571.
Wells, G. L., & Bradfield, A. L. (1998). "Good, you identified the suspect": Feedback to eyewitnesses distorts their reports of the witnessing experience. *Journal of Applied Psychology, 83*, 360–376.
Wells, G. L., Olson, E. A., & Charman, S. D. (2002). The confidence of eyewitness in their identifications from lineups. *Current Directions in Psychological Science, 11*, 151–154.
Wessel, I., van der Kooy, P., & Merckelbach, H. (2000). Differential recall of central and peripheral details of emotional slides is not a stable phenomenon. *Memory, 8*, 95–100.
Wright, D. B., & Stroud, J. N. (1998). Memory quality and misinformation for peripheral and central objects. *Legal and Criminological Psychology, 3*, 273–286.
Zaragoza, M. S. (1987). Memory, suggestibility, and eyewitness testimony in children and adults. In S. J. Ceci, M. P. Toglia, & D. F. Ross (Eds.), *Children's eyewitness memory* (pp. 53–78). New York: Springer-Verlang.
Zaragoza, M. S. (1991). Preschool children's susceptibility to memory impairment. In J. Doris (Ed.), *The suggestibility of children's recollections* (pp. 27–39). Washington DC: American Psychological Association.

Psychology Press
Taylor & Francis Group

Familiarity breeds distortion: The effects of media exposure on false reports concerning media coverage of the terrorist attacks in London on 7 July 2005

James Ost
University of Portsmouth, UK

Pär-Anders Granhag
Göteborg University, Sweden

Julie Udell
University of Portsmouth, UK

Emma Roos af Hjelmsäter
Göteborg University, Sweden

The present experiment investigated whether increased media exposure could lead to an increase in memory distortions regarding a traumatic public event: the explosion of the No. 30 bus in Tavistock Square, London on 7 July 2005. A total of 150 Swedish and 150 UK participants completed a series of questionnaires about their memory of either (i) the aftermath of the explosion, (ii) a non-existent computerised reconstruction of the moment of the explosion, or (iii) non-existent closed circuit television footage of the moment of the explosion. In line with the availability heuristic, UK participants were more likely than Swedish participants to claim to have seen all three types of footage. Furthermore, a sub-sample of UK participants who appeared to have developed false "memories" of seeing the No. 30 bus explode scored significantly higher on measures of dissociation and fantasy proneness than participants who did not develop false "memories". This experiment provides further support for the role of imaginative processes in the development of false memories.

Several studies have now shown that repeated suggestive interviews about parentally provided false childhood events leads a proportion of participants to claim that they actually remember experiencing such events (Loftus & Pickrell, 1995; Porter, Yuille, & Lehman, 1999; Wade, Garry, Read, & Lindsay, 2002). There is also evidence that asking participants to imagine non-events can change their subjective belief that such events actually occurred (Garry, Manning, Loftus, & Sherman, 1996; Mazzoni & Memon, 2003; but see Pezdek, Blandon-Gitlin, & Gabbay, 2006).

Hyman and Kleinknecht (1999) and Hyman and Loftus (1997) have proposed a three-stage model to explain how individuals might come to report that they remember events that did not occur. First, the person must believe that the event is plausible. Second, they must believe that

Address correspondence to: James Ost, Department of Psychology, University of Portsmouth, King Henry Building, King Henry I Street, Portsmouth, Hampshire, PO1 2DY, UK. Email: james.ost@port.ac.uk

The authors would like to thank Elke Geraerts, Marko Jelicic, and three anonymous reviewers for constructive comments which improved the quality of this paper. We would also like to thank Maria Dellenmark Blom for assistance with data collection.

http://www.psypress.com/memory DOI:10.1080/09658210701723323

they were likely to have experienced the event (see Scoboria, Mazzoni, Kirsch, & Relyea, 2004). Third they must make a source-monitoring error and misattribute the constructed memory as being a personal memory. Although there are important debates over terminology and the generalisability of findings (see DePrince, Allard, Oh, & Freyd, 2004; Pezdek & Lam, 2007; Wade et al., 2007; see also Smeets, Merckelbach, Horselenberg, & Jelicic, 2005) the convergent evidence suggests that a proportion of individuals will come to report that they remember witnessing events that they did not experience, or will incorporate substantial amounts of incorrect detail into their memory reports.

A recent line of research that complements the above studies has shown that people can be misled to report that they remember central details of recent, public events that they could not possibly have witnessed. This so-called "crashing memories" method typically asks participants to state whether they have seen (non-existent) video footage of highly charged public events, for example, a plane crash in Amsterdam (Crombag, Wagenaar, & van Koppen, 1996) or the car crash in which Diana, Princess of Wales, Dodi Al-Fayed, and their driver were killed (Ost, Vrij, Costall, & Bull, 2002; see also Granhag, Strömwall, & Billings, 2003; Jelicic et al., 2006b; Ost, Hogbin, & Granhag, 2006; Smeets et al., 2006; Wilson & French, 2006).

The crashing memory effect appears to be robust, with between 36% and 66% of participants in any given study claiming to have seen the non-existent video footage (Wilson & French, 2006; but see Jelicic, Smeets, Candel, van Suijdam, & Merckelbach, 2006a), however these rates can be reduced by phrasing the misleading question in an unambiguous, rather than ambiguous, manner (Smeets et al., 2006). Yet in almost every study to date the participants have been residents of the country in which the focal event took place (the studies by Ost et al., 2006, and Wilson & French, 2006, are the only exceptions). Therefore it becomes very difficult to tell whether the crashing memory effect occurs simply because there is something about certain people that leads them to generate "false memories" or because participants are exposed to lots of media coverage concerning the events about which they are misled.

The explanation initially suggested by Crombag et al. (1996), and echoed by Jelicic et al. (2006b) is that the vivid and emotionally charged nature of the events may lead participants to make a metacognitive error by combining the misleading suggestion that such footage exists with memories of footage (e.g., of the aftermath) that was shown on television, or pictures shown in media outlets (e.g., newspapers), and judging the resultant representation as a memory of the events that they did not, in fact, witness (see Hyman & Loftus, 1997). If this is the case, then when participants have been exposed to a lot of footage of such events they may be more likely to be misled about them (see Nourkova, Bernstein, & Loftus, 2004). Possibly, then, the crashing memories effect could be explained with reference to the availability heuristic.

According to the availability heuristic (Tversky & Kahneman, 1973), having seen similar footage may increase participants' willingness to report seeing similar non-existent footage because the repeated media coverage means that they are fairly easily able to retrieve information/images concerning that event[1]. Catastrophic events typically result in a great deal of detailed discussion and analysis by media outlets in the country where the event occurred. It is easy to see how this may lead to general information or images about that event being easier to retrieve for participants in that country (or with access to that media). Our first hypothesis was that there would be higher rates of false reporting in samples of participants who had been exposed to more television/media coverage of these events than samples of participants who had not.

The next two aspects of the study addressed two enduring problems with many of the existing crashing memories studies. The first problem is that we cannot be certain whether participants are truly *remembering* the events, or merely reporting that they *believe* the events to have occurred (Scoboria et al., 2004; Smeets et al., 2005; see also Ost, 2003). Specifically, participants in the present study were asked whether they remembered whether the bus was moving or not. This was included in order to try to differentiate those participants who seemed to genuinely have falsely "remembered" the event (e.g., seemed to be "picturing" the event) from those who merely "believed" that they had (e.g., answered "yes",

[1] Belli, Winkielman, Read, Schwarz, and Lynn (1998), for example, found that participants who were able to retrieve 4 childhood memories rated their overall memorial abilities as better than participants who were asked to retrieve 12 childhood events (a more difficult task).

but provided no information that could not have been gained from other sources).

The second, related, problem is that we cannot be sure that participants are truly remembering the false footage (i.e., developing a false "memory") or whether they are instead making a source misattribution and confusing computerised reconstructions as being their personal memories of the events. In the present study we explored this by including a condition in which participants were asked whether they had seen a (non-existent) computerised reconstruction of the moment of the explosion. Given that this comparison has not been made in previous research, we made no predictions about the likely rates of false reports in each condition.

Finally, we investigated personality correlates of false reporting or false memory. A substantial body of work has found that participants who score highly on personality measures related to dissociation (Wright & Loftus, 1999) and fantasy proneness (Merckelbach, Horselenberg, & Muris, 2001) are more likely to make certain types of memory errors (Geraerts, Smeets, Jelicic, van Heerden, & Merckelbach, 2005; Horselenberg et al., 2006; Ost et al., 2005; Wilson & French, 2006; Wright & Livingston-Raper, 2001; Wright & Osborne, 2005; but see Horselenberg, Merckelbach, van Breukelen, & Wessel, 2004).

METHOD

The target event

The target event was the explosion on the number 30 bus in Tavistock Square, London, on 7 July 2005. This was the fourth and final explosion on the morning of 7 July and occurred at approximately 09:50 British Standard Time. The three previous explosions had occurred around 08:50 British Standard Time on trains just outside Liverpool Street and Edgeware Road stations, and on a train travelling between King's Cross and Russell Square. Shortly after the first three explosions occurred, television stations began covering the scenes, showing survivors emerging from the underground stations. The coverage continued throughout the day and the attacks were covered extensively as the lead news story for several days on the major news channels and in all the major newspapers in the UK. It is highly likely that any resident of the UK would have seen at least some part of the television coverage. These events were the lead news story on Swedish television on 7 and 8 July, and continued to be the mentioned for the next few days, but not as the headline story.

Design

This experiment employed a 2 (Location: UK; Sweden) × 3 (Type of footage: aftermath; computerised reconstruction; closed circuit television) independent groups design. Participants in the first condition were asked whether they remembered seeing the televised footage of the aftermath of the explosion of the number 30 bus in Tavistock Square on 7 July 2005 (7/7). Participants in the second condition were asked about their memory of having seen a computerised reconstruction of the explosion on television. Participants in the third condition were asked about their memory of having seen closed circuit television (CCTV) footage of the actual moment of the explosion. Neither CCTV footage, nor a computerised reconstruction, showing the moment of the explosion on the bus, has ever been shown.

Participants

UK sample. A total of 150 (non-psychology) students were recruited at a university "Freshers' Fair" event and systematically assigned to conditions (e.g., participant one completed condition one, participant two completed condition two etc.). Three participants did not report their gender. The rest of the sample consisted of 69 males and 78 females, aged from 18 to 70 years ($M = 20.54$, $SD = 5.46$). Participants were recruited by responding to a poster asking people to complete a questionnaire entitled "How well do you remember the television coverage of the London bombings?" in return for being entered into a draw to win various prizes (vouchers for a local music shop). Participants who indicated that they had been personally involved, or knew someone who had been personally involved in the 7/7 attacks were not asked to complete the questionnaires, but their details were still entered into the prize draw. The experiment was approved by the Psychology Department Research Ethics Committee.

Swedish sample. A total of 150 participants (non-psychology) were recruited in university cafes, libraries, and other social areas, and systematically assigned to condition. Of these participants, 17 did not report their gender and 1 did not report their age. Of the remaining participants there were 46 males and 87 females, aged from 18 to 42 years ($M = 23.01$, $SD = 3.59$). Participants took part in return for being entered into a draw to win various prizes (e.g., cinema tickets).

Materials

Three recall questionnaires were constructed. The first section of the questionnaire asked for demographic information, including whether the participant had been resident in the country (UK or Sweden) for the last 6 months (questionnaires from three UK participants and two Swedish participants were excluded for this reason). The second section of the questionnaire was identical except that participants were asked about their memory of having seen either (i) the televised aftermath of the explosion of the number 30 bus in Tavistock Square on 7 July 2005, (ii) a computerised reconstruction of the explosion on television, or (iii) closed circuit television (CCTV) footage of the actual moment of the explosion. Participants were then asked to circle either Yes or No. If they indicated "No" then they were asked to skip ahead to a later section. Participants who answered "Yes" were asked to complete additional questions concerning their memory of the footage they had seen (adapted from Wilson & French, 2006). For the purposes of the present paper only three questions are directly relevant. These were "How certain are you that you have seen the [*CCTV/Computerised reconstruction/Aftermath*] footage?" (*1 = very uncertain to 7 = very certain*), and an open-ended question that asked "Please briefly describe the sequence of events shown in the [*CCTV footage/ Computerised reconstruction/Aftermath footage*]". Participants in the CCTV footage and computerised reconstruction were also asked "In the [*CCTV footage/Computerised reconstruction*], was the bus moving at the moment of the explosion?" (*Yes, No, Can't remember*). The recall questionnaires were straightforward to translate and any linguistic ambiguities were resolved by the authors via email prior to data collection. Finally, all UK participants were also asked to complete the Dissociative Experiences Scale (DES-C; Wright & Loftus, 1999) and the Creative Experiences Questionnaire (CEQ; Merckelbach et al., 2001), presentation of which was counterbalanced[2].

Procedure

These data were collected in both the UK and Sweden during a 2-week period at the beginning of October 2005, approximately 3 months after the events of 7 July 2005. The investigator explained the nature of the questionnaire, and the events to which it pertained. If participants indicated that they had not been personally involved in the 7 July events, then they were presented with a questionnaire pack consisting of the recall questionnaire (aftermath, reconstruction, or CCTV depending on condition) and, for the UK sample only, the individual differences measures, to complete at their own pace. Once the questionnaires were completed, participants were thanked for their time and debriefed fully about the nature of the experiment. Once the nature of the deception had been revealed to participants in the reconstruction and CCTV conditions, they were asked to sign a second informed consent form to indicate their consent for their data to be used.

RESULTS

Differences in UK and Swedish samples

The Swedish sample were significantly older ($M = 23.01$ years, SD 3.50) than the UK sample ($M = 20.54$ years, SD 5.46) $t(295) = 4.59$, $p < .005$, and comprised significantly more females than males in the Swedish sample, χ^2 $(1) = 4.40$, $p < .05$. However, there were no effects of gender on rates of false reporting in either the Swedish, $t(131) = 1.15$, $p > .05$, or UK $t(145) = 0.59$, $p > .05$, samples. Neither were there any correlations between age and false reporting for either the Swedish (*Kendall's tau_b* = –.03, $p > .05$) or UK (*Kendall's tau_b* = –.02, $p > .05$) samples.

[2] These questionnaires were not distributed to the Swedish sample due to time constraints which precluded timely translation of the questionnaires from English.

Rates of false reports of having seen real and false footage: Sweden vs UK

The next analysis examined the number of participants in the Swedish sample, compared to the UK sample, who claimed to have seen either non-existent CCTV footage, a non-existent computerised reconstruction, or the televised footage of the aftermath of the attack on the number 30 bus in Tavistock Square on 7 July 2005. Across both samples, participants were most likely to claim to have seen the aftermath footage (67%), followed by the non-existent CCTV footage (28%), and the non-existent computerised reconstruction (17%).

As shown in Table 1, the type of footage participants claimed to have seen differed significantly as a function of their geographical location. Of the UK sample, 40% claimed to have seen the non-existent CCTV footage, compared to 16% of the Swedish sample, $\chi^2(1) = 7.14$, $p < .01$; 28% of the UK sample claimed to have seen a non-existent computerised reconstruction, compared to 6% of the Swedish sample, $\chi^2(1) = 8.57$, $p < .01$; while 84% of the UK sample claimed to have seen any footage of the aftermath, compared to 50% of the Swedish sample, $\chi^2(1) = 13.07$, $p < .001$.

As also shown in Table 1, there was a main effect of geographical location on certainty judgements, $F_1(1, 106) = 9.54$, $p < .005$, with Swedish participants reporting significantly less certainty that they had seen any of the types of footage ($M = 1.91$, $SD = 0.90$) than UK participants ($M = 2.85$, $SD = 1.01$). Interestingly, there were no significant differences in participants' certainty scores as a function of which type of footage they were asked about, $F_2(1, 106) = 2.85$, *ns*. The mean scores indicate that this lack of variation was unlikely to be due to floor or ceiling effects, as the lowest mean certainty score (Swedish participants, reconstruction condition) was 3.66 ($SD = 2.51$) on a 7-point scale, whereas the highest (UK participants, aftermath condition) was 6.23 ($SD = 1.28$).

Distinguishing false "memories" from false "reports"

The next analysis focused on whether it was possible to distinguish participants who had just falsely reported seeing the event (i.e., who did not really "remember" it), from those who genuinely seemed to have a false memory of the event. Participants who claimed to have seen the non-existent footage were divided into two groups based on their answers to a question about whether, in the footage they claimed to have seen, the bus was moving or not. This first group, which stated that the bus definitely was or was not moving (they ticked a "yes" or "no" box in response to a question about whether or not the bus was moving at the moment of the explosion), were compared to participants who claimed that they could not remember this information (they ticked a "can't remember" box in answer to the same question). The reason for this split was to attempt to categorise participants who genuinely thought they had seen the footage from those participants who claimed to have seen it yet could not provide any further information about the footage. Of the 11 Swedish participants who claimed to have seen either the CCTV ($n = 8$) or reconstruction ($n = 3$), only 3 stated definitely that the bus was *not* moving (none claimed it was moving). Of the 34 UK participants who claimed to have seen the CCTV ($n = 20$) or reconstruction ($n = 14$), 12 stated that the bus was ($n = 3$), or was not ($n = 9$), moving.

Taking the base rates of exposure to media surrounding the events of 7 July into account allowed us to calculate (tentatively) that, in the Swedish sample (where the base rate of exposure was 50%), the rate of false reporting was 16% and the rate of false "memory" was 6%. Likewise, for the UK sample (where the base rate of exposure was 84%), the false reporting rate was 29% and the false "memory" rate was 12%. This may indicate for the first time the ratio of "false reports" to false "memory" using the crashing memories paradigm.

In order to investigate possible individual differences between participants who had a false memory of the footage, compared to those who made a false report, the analysis was run again but this time only including the 34 UK participants who had completed the personality questionnaires (the Swedish participants did not complete the individual differences measures). There was a significant difference between the groups on both of the personality questionnaires. Participants who made definite judgements about whether the bus was moving or not ($n = 12$) scored significantly higher on the DES-C ($M = 46.93$, $SD = 14.37$) than participants who reported that they did not know whether the bus was

TABLE 1
UK and Swedish participants who claimed to have seen each type of footage

	Number of participants who claimed to have seen each type of footage (yes/no) with certainty ratings (1–7) (percentage /SD)											
	CCTV				*Reconstruction*				*Aftermath*			
	Yes	*Cert.*	*No*	*Cert.*	*Yes*	*Cert.*	*No*	*Cert.*	*Yes*	*Cert.*	*No*	*Cert.*
UK $N = 150$	20 (40)	4.80 (1.90)	30 (60)	— $n = 50$	14 (28)	4.78 (2.22)	36 (72)	— $n = 50$	42 (84)	6.23 (1.28)	8 (16)	— $n = 50$
Sweden $N = 150$	8 (16)	3.75 (1.83)	42 (84)	— $n = 50$	3 (6)	3.66 (2.51)	47 (94)	— $n = 50$	25 (50)	4.08 (1.89)	25 (50)	— $n = 50$

Cert. refers to participants'' ratings of "certainty" (1 = very uncertain; 7 = very certain).

moving ($n = 22$, $M = 34.77$, $SD = 13.80$) $t(32) = 1.78$, $p < .05$, *one-tailed.* An effect in the same direction was found for participants' scores on the Creative Experiences Scale, with participants who claimed that the bus was, or was not, moving scoring significantly higher ($M = 13.33$, $SD = 4.22$) than participants who claimed that they did not remember ($M = 10.54$, $SD = 4.40$) $t(31) = 2.39$, $p < .05$, *one-tailed.* As shown below, the descriptions provided by these participants support the idea that these participants were making erroneous judgements of having seen the non-existent footage on the basis of a mental image of the sequence of events (i.e., a false "memory").

> Examples of participants' responses to open-ended statements about the sequence of events in the non-existent footage:
>
> "Bus appears to turn into Tavistock Square and people stand to get off and there is a flash and then nothing" (Participant 158).
>
> "The event was shown after a brief report. The bus has stopped at a traffic light. There was a bright light and a loud bang and the top of the bus flew off and lots of screaming and then everything seemed still" (Participant 13).
>
> "Bus had just stopped to let people off when two women got on and a man. He placed the bag by his side, the woman sat down and the doors closed, as the bus left there was the explosion and everyone started to scream while a leg was on the floor" (Participant 9).
>
> "The bus was moving slowly in traffic and then the back of the bus exploded. A lot of debris everywhere and people panicking" (Participant 131).
>
> "Bus moving normally, then explosion, debris everywhere, chaos" (Participant 24).

DISCUSSION

The present study replicated previous work showing that participants will claim to remember events that they were not exposed to (Crombag et al., 1996; Granhag et al., 2003; Ost et al., 2002; Ost et al., 2006; Jelicic et al., 2006b; Smeets et al., 2006; Wilson & French, 2006). More noteworthy are several important findings that extend our understanding of this kind of memory distortion.

In the present study 40% of UK participants and 16% of Swedish participants claimed to have seen a central aspect of a real-life traumatic event that they could not have witnessed. A smaller percentage (28% UK and 6% Swedish) claimed to have seen a computerised reconstruction of the moment of the explosion. The extent of false reporting was contingent on geographical location, with more UK participants (34%) in total claiming to have seen non-existent footage (CCTV + computerised reconstruction) than Swedish participants (11%). In line with the availability heuristic (Tversky & Kahneman, 1973) UK participants, who had been exposed to more media information about the attacks, were more prone to misremember a central detail such as having seen non-existent CCTV footage or a computerised reconstruction of the moment of the explosion. This is the first time the effect has been demonstrated using the crashing memories method—it would therefore be premature to conclude that the higher amounts of available information in the UK alone led to participants falsely reporting.

We cannot, for example, rule out the possibility that the higher personal salience of these events for the UK sample may well have led them to seek out further sources of information concerning the attacks (the UK sample were more likely to have had relatives working in London at the time, for example). The problem is that exposure and salience are likely to be highly positively correlated (the more salient an event is to you, the more likely you will be to seek information about it) which makes it difficult to analyse the effects of these two factors separately.

One possible way to examine this issue might be to find an event that was highly salient for a large number of individuals, some of whom had experienced more media exposure than others due to being in different geographical locations. For example, Schuster et al. (2001) conducted a random telephone survey of 560 US citizens in the days after the terrorist attacks on 11 September 2001. They found that the greatest stress reactions were reported by participants resident in New York at the time of the attacks, but that substantial stress symptoms were reported by respondents from all across the US. Following this line of thought, future studies might compare the memory errors of British nationals living abroad, participants resident in other areas of the UK, and participants who were resident in London at the time of the attacks. In this way the personal salience of the event might be held constant, while the geographical distance was varied. It might even be possible to examine, with appropriate ethical safeguards, memory errors (or lack thereof) in participants who were directly caught up in the events of 7 July 2005 (see Thompson, Morton & Fraser, 1997; Yuille & Cutshall, 1986).

False "memories" or false "reports"?

A recent debate in the false memory literature has focused on whether memory errors or distortions produced following certain methodologies can indeed be said to represent false memories (DePrince et al., 2004; Ost, 2003; Pezdek & Lam, 2007; Scoboria et al., 2004; Smeets et al., 2005; Wade et al., 2007). As noted by these authors, it is not always clear whether participants in some false memory studies actually "remember" a particular false event, or just "believe" they have seen it (Scoboria et al., 2004; Smeets et al., 2005; Ost, 2003; see also Tulving, 1989). The present data provided a partial solution to this problem. In the present experiment participants were asked whether they remembered the bus moving at the time of the explosion (response options: "yes", "no", and "can't remember"). Participants' responses to one closed question (which asked them whether or not the bus was moving at the time of the explosion) and a separate open-ended question (which asked them to describe the sequence of events in the non-existent CCTV footage) revealed that some participants reported having clear memories of the bus moving, and the subsequent explosion. As they clearly cannot have experienced these events, it is reasonable to assume that these descriptions must be the result of a false memory mechanism (Hyman & Kleinknecht, 1999; Hyman & Loftus, 1997). It is worth stressing again that the explosion was a central feature of the event that these participants *could not* have witnessed. Interestingly, participants who claimed to have seen the bus moving, compared to those who did not, scored significantly higher on measures of dissociation and measures of fantasy proneness (although this is not entirely surprising, given that both measures are highly correlated; Merckelbach, Muris, & Rassin, 1999). This suggests that these particular false memories are indeed likely to be the product of imaginative processes or a deficit and/or failure in metacognitive monitoring (Crombag et al., 1996).

It is important to note a number of caveats to our claims. First, participants who chose not to answer the question about the bus moving (e.g., who answered "don't know") might still have provided other (false) details of the CCTV if questioned further. Thus, it is conceivable that participants we classified as not having a false "memory" may indeed have developed a false "memory" about other aspects of the event, or may have believed that they had seen the footage but could not recall any specific details. They may also have incorrectly believed that the footage exists but that they either did not see it, or did see it but subsequently forgot about it. It is also possible that this group consisted of participants who "complied" with the initial question without ever believing the reality of the non-existent footage. In order to examine this possibility, future research should attempt to elicit narratives from participants (as opposed to yes/no responses) to examine in more detail the extent, or lack, of their memory errors. While we attempted to gather narrative details in the present study (by asking participants to give a brief description of the sequence of events), gathering more extended narratives would enable more detailed analyses. A second limitation is that we cannot rule out the possibility that some participants may already have believed that they had seen the non-existent footage before we suggested it to them. Thus it is not clear whether it is the misleading question that is driving this effect. One way this could be tested in the present methodology would be to pre-screen participants by eliciting a free narrative prior to any testing and then checking to see whether any false details were reported.

Summary

Our findings lend further support to the idea that it is relatively easy to mislead people to report incorrect central details concerning televised footage of highly charged public events. We found that, overall, Swedish participants were less likely to be misled than UK participants, even when we took base rates of exposure into account. Whether this is due primarily to increased exposure to images of the event from various media sources or due to other factors, such as the personal relevance of the event, remains an important question for future research. We were also able to suggest, for the first time, that the rate of false "memory" was roughly a third that of the rate of false reporting. Finally, we are able to show that the people most "at risk" of developing such false "memories" were those who scored higher on measures of dissociation and fantasy proneness. This clearly has important implications for the treatment of individuals in extended, abuse-focused therapy, and for the interviewing of witnesses to criminal events more generally.

First published online 2 November 2007

REFERENCES

Belli, R. F., Winkielman, P., Read, J. D., Schwarz, N., & Lynn, S. J. (1998). Recalling more childhood events leads to judgments of poorer memory: Implications for the recovered false memory debate. *Psychonomic Bulletin & Review, 5*, 318–323.

Crombag, H. F. M., Wagenaar, W. A., & van Koppen, P. J. (1996). Crashing memories and the problem of "source monitoring". *Applied Cognitive Psychology, 10*, 95–104.

DePrince, A. P., Allard, C. B., Oh, H., & Freyd, J. J. (2004). What's in a name for memory errors? Implications and ethical issues arising from the use of the term "false memory" for errors in memory for details. *Ethics & Behavior, 14*, 201–233.

Garry, M., Manning, C. G., Loftus, E. F., & Sherman, S. J. (1996). Imagination inflation: Imagining a childhood event inflates confidence that it occurred. *Psychological Bulletin and Review, 3*, 208–214.

Geraerts, E., Smeets, E., Jelicic, M., van Heerden, J., & Merckelbach, H. (2005). Fantasy proneness, but not self-reported trauma is related to DRM performance of women reporting recovered memories of childhood sexual abuse. *Consciousness and Cognition, 14*, 602–612.

Granhag, P-A., Strömwall, L., & Billings, F. J. (2003). "I'll never forget the sinking ferry": How social influence makes false memories surface. In M. Vanderhallen, G. Vervaeke, P. J. van Koppen, & J. Goethals (Eds.), *Much ado about crime: Chapters on psychology and law* (pp. 129–140). Belgium: Uitgeverij Politeia.

Horselenberg, R., Merckelbach, H., Smeets, T., Franssens, D., Peters, G. J. Y., & Zeles, G. (2006). False confessions in the lab: Do plausibility and consequences matter? *Psychology, Crime and Law, 12*, 61–75.

Horselenberg, R., Merckelbach, H., van Breukelen, G., & Wessel, I. (2004). Individual differences in the accuracy of autobiographical memory. *Clinical Psychology and Psychotherapy, 11*, 168–176.

Hyman, I. E., & Loftus, E. F. (1997). Some people recover memories of childhood trauma that never really happened. In P. S. Applebaum, L. A. Uyehara, & M. R. Elin (Eds.), *Trauma and memory: Clinical and legal controversies* (pp. 3–24). New York: Oxford University Press.

Hyman, I. E. Jr., & Kleinknecht, E. (1999). False childhood memories: Research, theory, and applications. In L. M. Williams & V. L. Banyard (Eds.), *Trauma and memory* (pp. 175–188). Thousand Oaks, CA: Sage.

Jelicic, M., Smeets, T., Candel, I., van Suijdam, M., & Merckelbach, H. (2006a). No, I don't remember seeing video footage of the killing of Theo van Gogh! Misinformation manipulations do not always elicit false memories. In K. Nixon (Ed.), *Forensic recall and eyewitness testimony* (pp. 21–25). London, UK: IA-IP Publishing.

Jelicic, M., Smeets, T., Peters, M. J. V., Candel, I., Horselenberg, R., & Merckelbach, H. (2006b). Assassination of a controversial politician: Remembering details from another non-existent film. *Applied Cognitive Psychology, 20*, 591–596.

Loftus, E. F., & Pickrell, J. E. (1995). The formation of false memories. *Psychiatric Annals, 25*, 720–725.

Mazzoni, G., & Memon, A. (2003). The effect of imagination on autobiographical beliefs and memories. *Psychological Science, 14*, 186–188.

Merckelbach, H., Horselenberg, R., & Muris, P. (2001). The Creative Experience Questionnaire (CEQ): A brief self-report measure of fantasy proneness. *Personality and Individual Differences, 31*, 987–995.

Merckelbach, H., Muris, P., & Rassin, E. (1999). Fantasy proneness and cognitive failures as correlates of dissociative experiences. *Personality and Individual Differences, 26*, 961–967.

Nourkova, V., Bernstein, D. M., & Loftus, E. F. (2004). Altering traumatic memory. *Cognition & Emotion, 18*, 575–585.

Ost, J. (2003). Essay review: Seeking the middle ground in the 'memory wars'. *British Journal of Psychology, 94*, 125–139.

Ost, J., Foster, S., Costall, A., & Bull, R. (2005). False reports of childhood events in appropriate interviews. *Memory, 13*, 700–710.

Ost, J., Hogbin, I., & Granhag, P-A. (2006). Altering false reports via confederate influence. *Social Influence, 1*, 105–116.

Ost, J., Vrij, A., Costall, A., & Bull, R. (2002). Crashing memories and reality monitoring: Distinguishing between perceptions, imaginings and false memories. *Applied Cognitive Psychology, 16*, 125–134.

Pezdek, K., Blandon-Gitlin, I., & Gabbay, P. (2006). Imagination and memory: Does imagining implausible events lead to false autobiographical memories? *Psychonomic Bulletin & Review, 13*, 764–769.

Pezdek, K., & Lam, S. (2007). What research paradigms have cognitive psychologists used to study "false memory", and what are the implications of these choices? *Consciousness & Cognition, 16*, 2–17.

Porter, S., Yuille, J. C., & Lehman, D. R. (1999). The nature of real, implanted, and fabricated memories for emotional childhood events: Implications for the

recovered memory debate. *Law and Human Behavior, 23*, 517–537.
Schuster, M. A., Stein, B. D., Jaycox, L. H., Collins, R. L., Marshall, G. N., Elliott, M. N., et al. (2001). A national survey of stress reactions after the September 11, 2001, terrorist attacks. *New England Journal of Medicine, 345*, 1507–1512.
Scoboria, A., Mazzoni, G., Kirsch, I., & Relyea, M. (2004). Plausibility and belief in autobiographical memory. *Applied Cognitive Psychology, 18*, 791–807.
Smeets, T., Jelicic, M., Peters, M. J. V., Candel, I., Horselenberg, R., & Merckelbach, H. (2006). "Of course I remember seeing that film!" – How ambiguous questions generate crashing memories. *Applied Cognitive Psychology, 20*, 779–789.
Smeets, T., Merckelbach, H., Horselenberg, R., & Jelicic, M. (2005). Trying to recollect past events: Confidence, beliefs, and memories. *Clinical Psychology Review, 25*, 917–934.
Thompson, J., Morton, J., & Fraser, L. (1997). Memories for the *Marchioness. Memory, 5*, 615–638.
Tulving, E. (1989). Memory: Performance, knowledge, and experience. *European Journal of Cognitive Psychology, 1*, 3–26.
Tversky, A., & Kahneman, D. (1973). Availability: A heuristic for judging frequency and probability. *Cognitive Psychology, 5*, 207–232.
Wade, K. A., Garry, M., Read, J. D., & Lindsay, D. S. (2002). A picture is worth a thousand lies: Using false photographs to create false childhood memories. *Psychonomic Bulletin and Review, 9*, 597–603.
Wade, K. A., Sharman, S. J., Garry, M., Memon, A., Mazzoni, G., Merckelbach, H., et al. (2007). False claims about false memory research. *Consciousness & Cognition, 16*, 18–28.
Wilson, K., & French, C. C. (2006). The relationship between susceptibility to false memories, dissociativity, and paranormal belief and experience. *Personality and Individual Differences, 41*, 1493–1502.
Wright, D. B., & Livingston-Raper, D. (2001). Memory distortion and dissociation: Exploring the relationship in a non-clinical sample. *Journal of Trauma and Dissociation, 3*, 97–109.
Wright, D. B., & Loftus, E. F. (1999). Measuring dissociation: Comparison of alternative forms of the dissociative experiences scale. *American Journal of Psychology, 112*, 497–519.
Wright, D. B., & Osborne, J. E. (2005). Dissociation, cognitive failures, and working memory. *American Journal of Psychology, 118*, 103–113.
Yuille, J. C., & Cutshall, J. L. (1986). A case study of eyewitness memory of a crime. *Journal of Applied Psychology, 71*, 291–301.

Aims and Scope of *Memory*

Memory publishes high quality research in all areas of memory research. This includes experimental studies of memory (including laboratory-based research, everyday memory studies and applied memory research), developmental, educational, neuropsychological, clinical and social research on memory. By representing all significant areas of memory research, the journal cuts across the traditional distinctions of psychological research. *Memory* therefore provides a unique venue for memory researchers to communicate their findings and ideas both to peers within their own research tradition in the study of memory, and also to the wider range of research communities with direct interest in human memory.

Memory is published by Psychology Press, an imprint of the Taylor & Francis Group, an Informa business. Correspondence for the publisher should be addressed to the Head Office, Psychology Press, 27 Church Road, Hove, East Sussex BN3 2FA, UK.

New subscriptions and changes of address should be sent to Psychology Press, T&F Customer Services, Informa UK Ltd, Sheepen Place, Colchester, Essex, CO3 3LP, UK. Tel: +44 (0) 20 7017 5544. E-mail: tf.enquiries@tfinforma.com. Please send change of address notices at least six weeks in advance, and include both old and new addresses.

Subscription rates to Volume 16, 2008 (8 issues) are as follows:
To institutions (full subscription): £661.00 (UK); €873.00 (Europe); $1,091.00 (Rest of World).
To institutions (online only): £627.00 (UK); €829.00 (Europe); $1,036.00 (Rest of World).
An institutional subscription to the print edition also includes free access to the online edition for any number of concurrent users across a local area network.
There is also a personal (print only) rate available which is strictly for personal, non-commercial use only. The reselling of personal subscriptions is strictly prohibited. Personal subscriptions must be purchased with a personal cheque or credit card and must be received at a personal (private) address. Personal subscribers may purchase a maximum of 4 subscriptions. Proof of personal status may be requested. For full information please visit the Journal's homepage.
To individuals: £319.00 (UK); €422.00 (Europe); $527.00 (Rest of World).
***Memory* (USPS permit number 016165)** is published in January, February, April, May, July, August, October, and November. The 2008 US institutional subscription price is $1,091.00. Periodicals Postage Paid at Jamaica, NY by US Mailing Agent Air Business Ltd, C/O Priority Airfreight NY Ltd, 147-29 182nd Street, Jamaica, NY 11413, USA. **US Postmaster:** Please send address changes to Air Business Ltd, C/O Priority Airfreight NY Ltd, 147-29 182nd Street, Jamaica, NY 11413, USA.

Memory is available online: please visit the journal website at http://www.psypress.com/memory

Memory is covered by the following abstracting, indexing and citation services: Biobase; Current Contents (ISI); Embase; Ergonomics Abstracts; Focus on Cognitive Psychology; LLBA; MEDLINE; PsycINFO; Research Alert; SciSearch; Social Sciences Citation Index; Sociological Abstracts; SCOPUS.

Back issues: Taylor & Francis retains a three-year back issue stock of journals. Older volumes are held by our official stockists: Periodicals Service Company, 11 Main Street, Germantown, NY 12526, USA to whom all orders and enquiries should be addressed. Tel: +1 518 537 4700; Fax: +1 518 537 5899; E-mail: psc@periodicals.com; URL: http://www.periodicals.com/tandf.html

Typeset by Datapage International Limited, Dublin, Ireland

Notes to Authors

MANUSCRIPT SUBMISSION

When possible, authors should submit their paper electronically. The paper should be a Word document or PDF—submissions in other formats cannot be processed. Please e-mail the paper as an attachment, providing full contact details of the corresponding author. This should be sent to **memory@leeds.ac.uk**. Alternatively authors should submit four copies of their paper, typed throughout in double space with wide margins. Submission of a paper is taken as acceptance by the author that it contains nothing libellous or infringes copyright. When a paper is accepted for publication, the copyright will belong to the publisher. Manuscripts should be sent to Susan E. Gathercole and Martin A. Conway, Editors of *Memory*, at the Institute of Psychological Sciences, The University of Leeds, Leeds LS2 9JT, UK.

FORMAT

Papers should be prepared in the format prescribed by the *American Psychological Association*. For full details of this format, please See the Publication Manual of the *APA* (5th edition).

Title. This should be as concise as possible, and typed on a separate sheet, together with the name(s) of the author(s) and the full postal address(es) of their institution(s). Proofs and requests for offprints will be sent to the first author unless otherwise indicated. A short running title of not more than 40 characters (including spaces) should also be indicated if the title is longer than this.

Abstract. An abstract of 100–150 words should follow the title page on a separate sheet.

Headings. Indicate headings and sub headings for different sections of the paper clearly. Do not number headings.

Acknowledgements. These should be as brief as possible and typed on a separate sheet at the beginning of the text.

Permission to quote. Any direct quotation, regardless of length, must be accompanied by a reference citation that includes a page number. Any quote over six manuscript lines should have formal written permission to quote from the copyright owner. It is the author's responsibility to determine whether permission is required from the copyright owner and, if so, to obtain it.

Footnotes. These should be avoided unless absolutely necessary. Essential footnotes should be indicated by superscript figures in the text and collected on a separate sheet at the end of the manuscript.

Reference citations within the text. Use authors' last names, with the year of publication in parentheses after the last author's name, e.g.: "Jones and Smith (1987)"; alternatively: "(Brown, 1982; Jones & Smith, 1987; White, Johnson, & Thomas, 1990)". On first citation of references with three or more authors, give all names in full, thereafter use first author "et al.". If more than one article by the same author(s) in the same year is cited, the letters a, b, c etc. should follow the year.

Reference list. A full list of references quoted in the text should be given at the end of the paper in alphabetical order of authors' surnames (or chronologically for a group of references by the same authors), commencing as a new sheet, typed double spaced. Titles of journals and books should be given in full, e.g.:

Books:

Cronbach, L. J., & Gleser, G. C. (1965). *Psychological tests and personnel decisions* (2nd ed.). Urbana, IL: Glencoe Press.

Chapter in edited book:

Jones, R. R., Reid, J. B., & Patterson, G. R. (1975). Naturalistic observation in clinical assessment. In P. McReynolds (Ed.), *Advances in psychological assessment* (Vol. 3, pp. 234–297). San Francisco, CA: Jossey-Bass.

Journal article:

Ellis, H. D., Lewis, M. B., Moselhy, H. F., & Young, A. W. (2000). Automatic without autonomic responses to familiar faces: Capgras delusion differentiates components of face recognition. *Cognitive Neuropsychology, 5,* 255–269.

If a paper is in preparation, submitted, or under review, the reference should include the authors, the title, and the year of the draft (the paper should also be cited throughout using the year of the draft). Manuscripts that are in press should also include the publisher or journal, and should substitute "in press" for the date (and should be cited as "in press"). The list of references should be typed with double spacing, and in alphabetical order of authors' name.

For Product Safety Concerns and Information please contact our EU representative GPSR@taylorandfrancis.com Taylor & Francis Verlag GmbH, Kaufingerstraße 24, 80331 München, Germany

Batch number: 10732718

Printed by Printforce, the Netherlands